REBALANCING
SOCIETY

HENRY MINTZBERG

REBALANCING SOCIETY

RADICAL RENEWAL BEYOND LEFT, RIGHT, AND CENTER

Berrett–Koehler Publishers, Inc.
a BK Currents book

Berrett-Koehler Publishers, Inc.
1333 Broadway, Suite 1000
Oakland, CA 94612-1921
Tel: (510) 817-2277   Fax: (510) 817-2278   www.bkconnection.com

Ordering Information

Quantity sales. Special discounts are available on quantity purchases by corporations, associations, and others. For details, contact the "Special Sales Department" at the Berrett-Koehler address above.

Individual sales. Berrett-Koehler publications are available through most bookstores. They can also be ordered directly from Berrett-Koehler: Tel: (800) 929-2929; Fax: (802) 864-7626; www.bkconnection.com

Orders for college textbook/course adoption use. Please contact Berrett-Koehler: Tel: (800) 929-2929; Fax: (802) 864-7626.

Orders by U.S. trade bookstores and wholesalers. Please contact Ingram Publisher Services, Tel: (800) 509-4887; Fax: (800) 838-1149; E-mail: customer.service@ingrampublisherservices.com; or visit www.ingrampublisherservices.com/Ordering for details about electronic ordering.

Berrett-Koehler and the BK logo are registered trademarks of Berrett-Koehler Publishers, Inc.

Printed in the United States of America

Berrett-Koehler books are printed on long-lasting acid-free paper. When it is available, we choose paper that has been manufactured by environmentally responsible processes. These may include using trees grown in sustainable forests, incorporating recycled paper, minimizing chlorine in bleaching, or recycling the energy produced at the paper mill.

Production Management: Michael Bass Associates
Cover Design: Archie Ferguson

Library of Congress Cataloging-in-Publication Data
Mintzberg, Henry.
   Rebalancing society : radical renewal beyond left, right, and center / Henry Mintzberg. — First edition.
       pages   cm.
   Includes bibliographical references and index.
   ISBN 978-1-62656-317-9 (pbk.)
   1. Corporate state. 2. Democracy. 3. Capitalism—Social aspects.
4. Civil society. I. Title.
   JC478.M56 2015
   306.3--dc23
                                                    2014035754

First Edition
19 18 17 16 15 14   10 9 8 7 6 5 4 3 2 1

I dedicate this book to those from whom we have borrowed this Earth, in the hope that they will be smarter than we have been.

Contents

Contents

The Basic Point

Enough!

Enough of the imbalance that is destroying our democracies, our planet, and ourselves.

Enough of the pendulum politics of left and right, as well as the paralysis in the political center. Enough of the visible claw of lobbying in place of the invisible hand of competing. Enough of the economic globalization that undermines sovereign states and local communities. Have we not had enough exploiting of the world's resources, including ourselves as "human resources"?

Many more people are concerned about these problems than have taken to the streets. The will of people is there; an appreciation of what is happening, and how to deal with it, is not. We are inundated with conflicting explanations and contradictory solutions. The world we live in needs a form of radical renewal unprecedented in the human experience. This book presents an integrative framework to suggest a comprehensive way forward.

The Triumph of Imbalance

When the communist regimes of Eastern Europe began to collapse in 1989, pundits in the West had a ready explanation: capitalism had triumphed. They were dead wrong, and the consequences are now proving fateful.

It was balance that triumphed in 1989. While those communist regimes were severely out of balance, with so much power concentrated in their public sectors, the successful countries of the West maintained sufficient balance across their public, private, and what can be called plural sectors. But a failure to understand this point has been throwing many countries out of balance ever since, in favor of their private sectors.

Welcome to the Plural Sector

There are three consequential sectors in society, not two. The one least understood is known by a variety of inadequate labels, including the "not-for-profit sector," the "third sector," and "civil society." Calling it "plural" can help it take its place alongside the ones called public and private, while indicating that it is made up of a wide variety of human associations.

Consider all those associations that are neither public nor private—owned neither by the state nor by private investors—such as foundations, places of worship, unions, cooperatives, Greenpeace, the Red Cross, and many renowned universities and hospitals. Some are owned by their members; most are owned by no one. Included here, too, are social movements that arise to protest what some people find unacceptable (as we have seen recently in the Middle East) and social initiatives, usually started by small community groups, to bring about some change they feel is necessary (for example, in renewable energy).

Despite the prominence of all this activity, the plural sector remains surprisingly obscure, having been ignored for so long in the great debates over left versus right. This sector cannot be found between the other two, as if on some straight line. It is a different place, as different from the private and public sectors as these two are from each other. So picture instead a balanced society as sitting on a stool with three sturdy legs: a public sector of respected governments, to provide many of our protections (such as policing and regulating); a private sector of responsible businesses, to supply many of our goods and services; and a plural sector of robust communities, wherein we find many of our social affiliations.

Regaining Balance

How do we regain balance in our societies? Some people believe that the answer lies in the private sector—specifically, with greater corporate social responsibility. We certainly need more of this, but anyone who believes that corporate social responsibility will compensate for corporate social irresponsibility is living in a win-win wonderland. Other people expect democratic governments to act vigorously. This they must do, but they will not so long as public states continue to be dominated by private entitlements, domestic and global.

This leaves but one sector, the plural, which is not made up of "them" but of you, and me, and we, acting together. We shall have to engage in many more social movements and social initiatives, to challenge destructive practices and replace them with constructive ones. We need to cease being human resources, in the service of imbalance, and instead tap our resourcefulness as human beings, in the service of our progeny and our planet.

1

The Triumph
of Imbalance

A SOCIETY OUT OF BALANCE, with power concentrated in
a privileged elite, can be ripe for revolution. The American
colonies by 1776 were ripe for revolution, as was Russia in
the early twentieth century. So are many countries today,
including some called democratic.

The trouble with revolution is that it usually replaces
one form of imbalance with another. As some people
among the disenfranchised gain power through force, they
tend to carry their society toward some new extreme.
Lenin promised the Russian people a "dictatorship of the
proletariat." Instead, their revolution brought them a
dictatorship of the Communist Party, exercised through
the public sector. This new regime may have attended
to certain collective needs, but at the expense of individual liberties. The United States went the other way,
although it took two hundred years before tipping into
imbalance.

America's Long March Toward Imbalance: 1789–1989

The seeds of this imbalance were sown in the American Revolution. **America did not invent democracy so much as give impetus to a particularly individualistic form of it.** The people revolted against the authoritarian rule of the British monarchy and thus wrote "checks and balances" into their constitution. While these checked the power of government, by ensuring a certain balance across its executive, legislative, and judicial institutions, no such constitutional constraints checked the power of individuals and nonstate institutions.

As a consequence, the country thrived and became the world's model for development—social and political as well as economic. For individuals seeking opportunity as well as escape from tyranny, America became the place to go. Even for those who stayed home, it was the place to emulate.

But that model worked only so long as the country maintained some semblance of balance. The power of individuals and their private institutions had to be constrained. That responsibility fell to government, in the form of laws and regulations, as well as to communities that upheld the prevalent social norms.

With the weakening of both government and local communities in recent years, this balance has been lost. Yet the American model remains the favored one in much of the world. Accordingly, we had better understand what has been going on in the United States if we are to find our way to restored balance.

The Rise of the Corporation

The nonstate institutions of the United States are mainly of two types: private businesses—for-profit—and community and other associations—not-for-profit. In his landmark study of *Democracy in America in the 1830s*, Alexis de Tocqueville recognized the latter as not only quintessentially American but also key to the country's democracy (1840/2003: 115). He favored the word *associations*, but they were also referred to back then as "corporations," as were certain businesses. As the private sector gained increasing influence, however, the word *corporation* came to be associated more exclusively with businesses.

The U.S. Constitution made no mention of corporations, let alone granted them liberties. The liberties it affirmed were for individual persons, in the spirit of Thomas Jefferson's immortal words in the Declaration of Independence that "[w]e hold these truths to be self-evident, that all men are created equal." At the time, "men" meant all white and propertied males. These gender, color, and financial restrictions were eventually eliminated, but not before an 1886 ruling by the Supreme Court reinforced property rights with a vengeance: corporations were recognized as "persons" with "equal protection of the laws."[1] Granting them this equal protection has made all the difference. **From the liberties for individuals enshrined in the American Constitution sprang entitlements for private corporations.**

Thomas Jefferson and Abraham Lincoln were highly suspicious of these corporations. Jefferson hoped that "we shall crush . . . in its birth the aristocracy of our monied corporations, which dare already to challenge our government to a trial by strength." And Lincoln worried that "corporations have been enthroned" by the Civil War, so that wealth could be "aggregated in a few hands and the republic . . . destroyed. . . . God grant that my suspicions may prove groundless." God did not grant any such thing. Instead, twenty-two years later the Supreme Court granted corporations that personhood mentioned earlier.

This development happened amid the rise of the great business trusts—massive monopolies in oil, steel, and other industries, created by people who came to be called "robber barons." These trusts were eventually beaten back by the anti-trust legislation of 1890 and 1914, and imbalance was further held in check by President Franklin Roosevelt's New Deal enacted during the Great Depression of the 1930s as well as the welfare programs established after World War II. But underway at the same time was a "Cold War," during which American defense spending grew to equal that of the rest of the world combined. And so a third Republican president weighed in on the influence of corporations: Dwight David Eisenhower pointed to a "military-industrial complex" as having "the potential for the disastrous rise of misplaced power."

Supporting Dogma from Economics

Supporting this march toward imbalance has been an economic perspective that grew into a prevailing dogma (Hayek 1944; Friedman 1962). In its boldest form, **this dogma centers on an "economic man" for whom greed is good, property is sacred, markets are sufficient, and governments are suspect. As *one* view of human society, this makes some sense; as *the* view of human society, it is nonsense.**

4

But such nonsense did not stop the march toward imbalance; indeed, it expedited it, by providing formal justification for the corporate entitlements. Economics may be changing now—at the margins, at least—but the damage had been done: as greed became a cult, property rights were allowed to run rampant and many markets went out of control. In 1989, two hundred years after the U.S. Constitution had gone into effect, the stage was set for the country's free fall into imbalance.

The End of Thinking: 1989–___?

Communism, and the political left in general, had served as a modest constraint on capitalism, by harping on its weaknesses. But as the communist regimes of Eastern Europe began to collapse in 1989, this constraint also collapsed. After all, if governments under communism proved bad, then surely all governments themselves had to be constrained. **"Capitalism has triumphed!" declared Western pundits in 1989. They were wrong—dead wrong.**

The Berlin Wall was still standing when an article in the American magazine *National Interest*, under the title "The End of History?" (Fukuyama 1989—without the question mark in his 1992 book), declared capitalism to be not only the best system then, or even the best system ever, but the best system forever.

> What we may be witnessing is not just the end of the Cold War, or the passing of a particular period of post-war history, but the end of history as such: that is, the end point of mankind's ideological evolution and

the universalization of Western liberal democracy as the final form of human government. (p. 1)

Karl Marx's communism was declared dead, so long live Adam Smith's free markets, at least as depicted in one passage of his 1776 book about an "invisible hand" that drives butchers, brewers, and bakers—free men in the marketplace—to serve society by serving themselves. "It is not from the benevolence of the butcher, the brewer, or the baker, that we expect our dinner, but from their regard to their own interest." Mankind (for all of this was about that "economic man") had reached perfection, thanks to relentless greed. The floodgates to private power were now wide open.

Never mind that by 1989 Americans were receiving much of their meat, beer, and bread from giant corporations with paramount positions in their marketplaces. Never mind, too, that these corporations were able to exert significant influence over the lives of the many people who butchered, brewed, and baked for them, as well as over these people's governments. Adam Smith's world may have long since passed, but not the quaint belief in this one passage of his. **It was not history that had ended but thinking, as all we economic men and women were spared the burden of contemplating our future.**

Even by the standards of neoconservative America, Fukuyama's arrogance was monumental. But he was not alone. The moderate economist Paul Krugman, winner of one of those Bank of Sweden Prizes in Economic Sciences (erroneously called Nobel[2]), concurred under the subheading of a *Fortune* magazine article in 2000 that read, "Economic man is free at last": "both the American economy and the free-market system it epitomizes seem everywhere triumphant. . . . [A]ny future claims about a system that trumps the free market are going to face severe skepticism." Krugman added, all too prophetically:

> [P]olicy makers and the public are now willing . . . to stick with markets even when they misbehave. . . . [B]asically companies will be allowed to make money as best they can in the belief that the invisible hand will direct them to more or less the right place.

What both Krugman and Fukuyama failed to address is a simple question posed later by John Kay, an economist who kept thinking, "Did Marxism fail because it was the wrong grand design, or because all grand designs for economic systems are misconceived?" (2003: 192). Put differently, **might we social people be grander than economic theory?**

This book challenges the dogma that sees all of us driven to compete, collect, and consume our way to neurotic oblivion. That some of us choose to do so is indisputable. That many of us doing so poses a threat to our collective survival has likewise become indisputable. In place of this dogma, this book offers an integrating framework, built on our social, political, and economic predispositions, to consider how to restore balance in society.

Over the Edge: From 1989

In 1989, the United States of America was two hundred years old. The following words were themselves written two hundred years ago:

> The average age of the world's greatest civilizations has been 200 years. Great nations rise and fall. The people go from bondage to spiritual truth, to great courage, from courage to liberty, from liberty to abundance, from

abundance to selfishness, from selfishness to complacency, from complacency to apathy, from apathy to
dependence, from dependence back again to bondage.[3]

The United States had experienced many of these stages
by 1989, while retaining characteristics of each. Is a return
to bondage happening now?

**What triumphed in 1989, relatively speaking, was
balance.** The communist regimes of Eastern Europe were
severely out of balance, with so much power concentrated
in their public sectors. In contrast, the successful countries called Western exhibited a balance of power across
the three main sectors of society—public, private, and
plural—more or less.

More was the case in countries such as Germany and
Canada, less in the United States. Yet compared with
what came after 1989, the United States still mitigated
the forces of markets and individualism with extensive
public welfare services, substantial regulations of business, and significant taxation of wealthy individuals and
corporations. In fact, "America emerged from World War
II with government, market, and civil society [the plural
sector] working together in a healthier, more dynamic,
and more creative balance than at any time since pre–Civil
War years" (Korten 1995: 88).[4]

But a failure to understand this need for balance drove
the country over the tipping point, to imbalance. For if
capitalism had indeed triumphed, then the economists
had it right and the corporations were the heroes. They
had saved the world from the communist menace. But
if it was balance that had triumphed, then private sector
excesses needed to be stopped, right then and there. The
opposite happened: these excesses accelerated.

It is not that businesses have been waging some kind of orchestrated conspiracy. True, they have sometimes acted in concert to enhance their influence, as when their associations have lobbied for lower taxes. But of far greater effect has been the steady pull of so many private forces, each pursuing its own interests—for the creation of tax loopholes, extension of government subsidies, loosened enforcement of regulations, and so on—pitted against public agencies that have become less and less able, and inclined, to resist them.

Add up the consequences of so many deliberate but disparate actions—all the lobbying and litigating, maneuvering and manipulating—and the country has ended up with the equivalent of a coup d'état. **Adam Smith's invisible hand in the American marketplace has become a visible claw in the American Congress. De Tocqueville identified the genius of American society as "self-interest rightly understood." Now the country finds itself overwhelmed by self-interest fatefully misunderstood.**[5]

Consider the extent to which power has shifted in America since 1989—for example, the significant skewing of wealth to the richest 1 percent of the population and Supreme Court rulings that have opened the floodgates to political donations. "Only a generation ago, excluding corporations from the political arena was not only thinkable and debatable but was also the law in some [American] states" (Nace 2003: 233). Back in "the mid-1980s, President Ronald Reagan overhauled the tax system after learning that General Electric . . . was among dozens of corporations that had been using accounting gamesmanship to avoid paying taxes. 'I didn't realize that things had gotten that far out of line,'" he said (Kocieniewski 2011a). From 2008 to 2012, twenty-six major American corporations, including General Electric and Boeing, paid no federal income taxes at all (Drawbaugh and Temple-West 2014).

On the global front, with regard to the environment, the Montreal Protocol of 1987 dealt with the problem of the ozone layer, as a "result of unprecedented international cooperation" (Bruce 2012). Now we have been having conference after conference on global warming whose results would be laughable were the issue in question not so important.[6] (The appendix describes various aspects of our current state of imbalance.)

From Market Economy to Corporate Society

It has been said that the final stage of slavery is when you no longer realize that you are a slave. The East Europeans under communism never reached that stage. They understood full well how enslaved they were by their system of governance. But how many of us in so many countries now realize the extent to which we have become the slaves of our own economic structures? Do we recognize the extent to which our so-called market economies have become corporate societies, wherein business as usual has become hardly anything but business? **When an economy of free enterprise becomes a society of free enterprises, it's the citizens themselves who are no longer free.**[7]

As the Berlin Wall fell, it took with it much of the left side of the political spectrum of countries all over the world. Because the governments of Eastern Europe were discredited, people were persuaded to see all governments as discredited. This view has been especially prevalent where the population has long harbored suspicions about government. Suspicions are one thing; a collective misunderstanding of the role of government in a balanced society is quite another. Voters who thoughtlessly dismiss that role usually get the governments they deserve. (Articles of mine that elaborate on points in the text, such as this one, are listed in a section at the end of the references.)

It is telling that *socialism* has become a dirty word in America, leaving the impression that there is something wrong with things social, while *capitalism* has come to represent all things right. In fact, now we are seeing all kinds of proposals for *adjectival* capitalism—sustainable capitalism, caring capitalism, breakthrough capitalism, democratic capitalism, regenerative capitalism, inclusive capitalism. The implication is that, if only we can get capitalism right, all will be well again.

How did the word *capitalism*, coined to describe the creation and funding of private enterprises, themselves intended to supply us with commercial goods and services, come to represent the be-all and end-all of human existence? Is capitalism any way to run public services or judge their effectiveness, any way to understand the needs of education and health care, any way to organize our social lives and express our values as human beings? Capitalism was intended to serve us. Why are so many of us now serving it? Or as Pope Francis said recently, "Money must serve, not rule."

In the United States in particular, the private sector now dominates society to such an extent that no established form of political activity is likely to dislodge it. The restoration of balance will thus require some form of renewal unprecedented in American history.

Not Only in America

After I gave a talk on these ideas a couple of years ago, a Swede asked me why I placed so much emphasis on the United States. Surely countries like Sweden were more balanced.

Maybe so, I replied, but for how long? The United States may be leading the march to imbalance, but it is hardly marching alone. A great many countries are being thrown out of balance by the spreading influence of the economic dogma in cahoots with a globalization movement that is suppressing so many things local. In a surprising number of countries, the rich are getting exponentially richer while income levels for the rest are stagnating and social problems are festering. My own country, Canada, long known for its balance and benevolence, has become another cheerleader for this one-sided view of development. There is a creeping meanness in my country that I find alarming, led by, but not restricted to, our current government. If Canada has succumbed, can Sweden be far behind? (See the accompanying box.)

So no matter where you live, if you wish to sustain whatever balance remains in your own country and help stop what could be the end of our history, I suggest that you understand what is happening in the United States—especially if you are American. (A section at the end of the appendix presents some evidence about the state of democracy in America twenty-five years after this triumph of capitalism.)

Public Rights or Private Profits?

A number of recent bilateral trade pacts have included special courts of arbitration that enable private companies to sue sovereign states whose laws or regulations—even in matters relating to health, culture, and environment—they see as having reduced "the value of [their] profits or expected future profits" (Nace 2003: 257). Some corporations have used these courts not to sue states so much as to threaten them with such suits, which has had a "chilling effect on legislation" (Monbiot 2013).

In December 2013, the *New York Times* ran an article as well as an editorial discussing how "big tobacco" had been using such litigation to "intimidate" and "bully" poor countries around the world into rescinding regulations intended to control the use of tobacco. The health minister of Namibia reported receiving "'bundles and bundles of letters' from the industry about its attempts to curb smoking rates among young women" (Tavernise 2013). In reference to the North American Free Trade Agreement, one Canadian official likewise reported seeing "the letters from the New York and DC law firms coming up to the Canadian government on virtually every new environmental regulation and proposition in the last five years." One pharmaceutical company even "demand[ed] that Canada's patent laws be changed" (Monbiot 2013).

In his article about these courts of arbitration, referred to in the title as "a Full-frontal Assault on Democracy," George Monbiot wrote:

> The rules are enforced by panels which have none of the safeguards we expect in our own courts. The hearings are held in secret. The judges are corporate lawyers, many of whom work for companies of the kind whose cases they hear. Citizens and communities

affected by their decisions have no legal standing. There is no right of appeal.

One NGO labeled this "a privatized justice system for global corporations," while a judge on these courts was quoted as saying that "it never ceases to amaze me that sovereign states have agreed to [such] arbitration at all."

As I write this, the European Union is negotiating a trade pact with the United States. As a consequence, the lopsided lobbying so prevalent in the United States has come to Brussels with full force, a good deal of it from U.S. law firms (Lipton and Hakim 2013).[8] If they succeed in installing such a court of arbitration, these "negotiations could . . . become de facto global standards" (Hakim and Lipton 2013), given that the European Union and the United States account for almost half the world's trade.

If, however, the Europeans stand their ground, this could become a turning point that puts an end to such courts and encourages national courts to dismiss them as outrageous violations of their citizens' rights.

A Rant Against Imbalance, Not Business

If the text so far (and the appendix later) sounds like a rant, then let me assure you that it is—for good reason. We have had enough of all this.

But please do not take this as a rant against business. I cherish businesses that compete responsibly to bring me worthwhile products and services. I eat at wonderful restaurants, work with dedicated publishers, buy some strikingly creative products. I have deep respect for the companies that respect me. Thankfully there remain many of these, big and small.

But I have equally deep disdain for the companies that try to exploit me with shoddy products, indifferent services, bamboozled pricing, and phony advertising. These companies are on the increase, thanks to the relentless drive for growth expected of them by frenetic stock markets.

Likewise, I have deep disdain for those companies that seek to exploit *us*: by using political advertising to sway opinions on public issues, taking government handouts in the name of free enterprise, spending vast sums on lobbying to enhance their privileged positions. In 1952 in the United States, 32 percent of all taxes were paid by corporations; by 2010, that figure was down to 9 percent. **There's a tea party going on, all right, for big business, under the slogan "No taxation *with* representation."**

In his *Devil's Dictionary*, first published in 1906, Ambrose Bierce defined the corporation as "an ingenious device for obtaining individual profit without individual responsibility." Ingenious it may be, but can we continue to tolerate this? We turn next to a comparison of the world we have with a world that could be.

2

From Exploiting Resources to Exploring Our Resourcefulness

WE CAN EXPLOIT the world's resources, be they land, water, air, or the creatures that inhabit them, including ourselves as "human resources." Or we can explore our own natural resourcefulness.[9]

A World That Exploits Its Resources

Some enterprises explore—for example, to come up with innovative products. Others exploit, sometimes constructively—say, to bring us lower prices—other times destructively, by squeezing their workers, suppliers, and customers instead of building sustainable relationships with them. A healthy economy favors the explorers that serve themselves by serving us. Too many economies are now favoring the exploiters that serve themselves at the expense of us.

Witness the bailouts of some of the sickest companies alongside subsidies and tax breaks for some of the richest. Consider the revelations about fraud and other forms of corporate malfeasance that go unpunished. (If you wish to break the law and stay out of jail, I suggest you wear a white collar, not a blue one.) The problem is that by reinforcing their established positions, the exploiters are hogging too much of the world's wealth.

Don't look to the economists to fix this problem. They work in the upper reaches of abstract theories and aggregated statistics, while the economy functions on the ground, where products are made and customers are served. Here is where this problem is festering, in the mismanagement of so many large companies for the sake of quick bonuses. And so here is where the economy will have to be fixed, with patience and determination, enterprise by enterprise. (See "Rebuilding American Enterprise" on www.mintzberg .org/enterprise.)

Exploiting the Externalities

In a world of exploitation, I can do as I please with my property, any harmful social and environmental consequences be damned. The economists have a convenient word for these damned consequences: *externalities*. It means that while a few people gain from the tangible benefits of what they own, everyone else pays for the intangible costs—such as the air polluted by someone's factory and the mental breakdowns of the workers that company "downsizes." (This process of firing people in great numbers has become the bloodletting of our age—the cure for every corporate ill.)

But don't think it's just *them*. It's me, too. And you.

Take the simple example of garbage. Where I live, I can throw out as much as I like—that costs me nothing. Besides, recycling takes effort. Why should I bother?

The fatal flaw in this thinking is that **there are no human activities without externalities, and these are accumulating at unsustainable rates.** Garbage may be free for me, but it is not free for us. **What many of us can afford, our planet cannot: our micro behaviors are rendering macro destruction.**

Economists tell us that if we can afford it, we can do it: drive gas-guzzling cars, amass possessions beyond what we can possibly use, eat gluttonously while our neighbors go hungry. Supply and demand will take care of the problem. (Go tell that to a hungry neighbor.) So instead of stopping destructive practices, we try to price them to reduce demand. This idea is fundamentally perverse: only the rich are allowed to indulge. But what happens to life on Earth when so many of us can afford such indulgences while so many more are waiting to join the party? Will supply and demand kick in after it's too late? **Dig beneath these two foundations of economic theory—our right to consume whatever we can afford and to slough off the externalities—and have a look at the behaviors that are crawling underneath.**

Competitive markets are wonderful—so long as, in the spirit of Adam Smith, they serve the broader society. What we are seeing instead are *markets of entitlement*, which benefit some people at the expense of many others: markets for subprime mortgages, for executive compensation, for recycled aluminum. In a full-page investigative report in the *New York Times*, David Kocieniewski (2013a) described the "dance . . . choreographed by Goldman Sachs to exploit pricing regulations set up by an overseas commodity exchange" for recycled aluminum. In three years the company was reported to have extracted $5 billion out of that market simply by storing it and shifting it between warehouses. Imagine if such behaviors were treated as manipulative robbery instead of just legal corruption.

John Maynard Keynes famously declared, "In the long run, we are all dead." By "we" he meant each of us, not all of us: there is no collective *we* in mainstream economics. But it is the collective *we* that is now threatened—ecologically, politically, socially, even economically—and the long run is getting shorter.

In the name of liberty, we are suffering from individualism: every person and every institution striving to get the most for him-, her-, or itself, over the needs of society and a threatened planet.[10] Enough of the clever words of Keynes. We had better heed the wise words of Chief Seattle, the aboriginal elder who declared, "We do not inherit the earth from our ancestors; we borrow it from our children."

A World That Explores Our Resourcefulness

Have we not had enough of the "isms" that have empowered the few while marginalizing so many others? After royalism and feudalism came capitalism and communism, and later fascism. Now capitalism has become the end of history. Under Russian communism, the apparatchiks hijacked the country's "dictatorship of the proletariat"; now, under the current version of capitalism, the free enterprises are hijacking the democracy of free people. Both *communism* and *capitalism* are labels for systems that promote undeserved privilege. To reverse a pre-1989 Russian expression, "Communism is the exploitation of man by man. Capitalism is the opposite."

To paraphrase T. S. Eliot, we need to cease from exploitation so that we can arrive where we started and know our place for the first time. That will entail exploring our resourcefulness, individually and collectively. We human beings are in no small measure explorers—for creative ideas, not just crude oil. In fact, we are quite resourceful ones—to benefit ourselves, to be sure, but also for the greater good. Exploring can also render us more productive because, whereas exploitation exhausts our resources, exploration energizes our resourcefulness. (See the accompanying box.)

The Fresh Air of Resourcefulness

Mary Parker Follett presented a paper in 1925 about three ways to deal with conflict, only one of which she favored.

The first she called *domination*: the victory of one side over the other. The problem is that the other side "will simply wait for its chance to dominate." We have seen this way in various revolutions and see too much of it in our current imbalance. A second way she called *compromise*: "each side gives up a little in order to have peace." But with neither side satisfied, Follett concluded that the conflict will keep coming back. We have been seeing too much of this way, too.

Follett favored a third way, which she called *integration*: moving the debate to another place, getting back to basics to find common ground:

Integration involves invention . . . and the clever thing is to recognize this and not to let one's thinking stay within the boundaries of two alternatives which are mutually exclusive. In other words, never let yourself be bullied by an either-or situation. . . . Find a third way.

Follett used a simple example. She was in a small room in a library where someone wanted the window open, to get fresh air. But she wanted it closed, to avoid the draft. So they opened a window in the next room. This solution was hardly brilliant or creative, just resourceful. All it took were two open minds and some goodwill. We desperately need more such fresh air today.

In a robust economy, growth is judged by the qualities enhanced, not just measured by the quantities produced. Such an economy does not merely expand; it develops, qualitatively and socially. So—how to get to that?

3

Three Pillars to Support a Balanced Society

IN JAMES CLAVELL'S NOVEL *Shogun*, the Japanese woman tells her British lover, confused by the strange world into which he has been shipwrecked, "It's all so simple, Anjin-san. Just change your concept of the world." To regain balance, we, too, just have to change our concept of the world. A good place to start is by reframing the political dichotomy that for two centuries has narrowed our thinking along one straight line.

Left   Right

The Consequences of Left and Right

Since the late eighteenth century, when the commoners sat to the left of the speakers in the French legislatures and the *ancien régime* to the right, we have been mired in great debates over left versus right, states versus markets, nationalization versus privatization, communism versus capitalism, and on and on. A pox on both of these houses. We have had more than enough sliding back and forth between two unacceptable extremes.

Capitalism is not good because communism proved bad. Carried to their dogmatic limits, both are fatally flawed. "So long as the only choice is between a voracious market and a regulatory state, we will be stuck in a demoralizing downward spiral" (Bollier and Rowe 2011: 3). To put it in terms of contemporary politics, too many countries now swing fruitlessly between left and right, while others sit paralyzed in the political center.

Pendulum and Paralyzed Politics

It is surprising how many voters now line up obediently on one side or the other of the political spectrum. **Left or right, most voters see everything as black and white.** Discussion has given way to dismissal and trust to suspicion, while nastiness takes center stage.

It is even more surprising how many countries are split so evenly between such voters. "Between 1996 and 2004 [Americans] lived in a 50-50 nation in which the overall party vote totals barely budged five elections in a row" (Brooks 2011d).

In such elections, a few voters in the center determine the winner. They may want moderation, but by having to cast their votes one way or the other, they often get domination: the elected party carries the country far beyond what its vote justifies, to serve its minority while ignoring the majority, including some of the people who helped get it elected. Egyptians in 2012 got the Muslim Brotherhood, while Americans in 2000 who voted for George W. Bush's "compassionate conservatism" got his tragic war in Iraq.

These center voters eventually get fed up and switch—if they still have the choice—so the country ends up in pendulum politics: up goes the right and down goes the left, until up goes the left and down goes the right, as each side seeks to cancel the accomplishments of the other. Or else the country stays up on one side as the elected leader becomes a dictator.

Countries with larger numbers of moderate voters tend to get more moderate politics, with governments closer to the center. This may be a better place, with its penchant for compromise. But as Mary Parker Follett pointed out (see the box in Chapter 2), that place has its own problems. Coalitions of compromise, de facto or de jure, have to negotiate everything, left and right. The country can end up with micro solutions for its macro problems or, worse, fall into political gridlock.

Power to the Entitled

While politics gets gridlocked, or swings back and forth fruitlessly, **society itself is not disabled: private power proliferates.** As the politicians debate marginal changes in their parochial legislatures at home and offer lofty pronouncements at their grand conferences abroad, powerful corporations so inclined bolster their entitlements, by busting unions, reinforcing cartels, manipulating governments,[11] and escaping whatever taxes and regulations remain. All of this behavior is cheered on by economists who revel in such freedom of the marketplace, while the world tumbles into imbalance.

Protesting What Is While Confusing What Should Be

In recent years, protests have erupted in various parts of the world—for example, in the Middle East over dictatorships and in Brazil over corruption. The United States has experienced occupations from the left and Tea Parties from the right, both clearer about what they oppose than what to propose. For example, included in the "Non-negotiable Core Beliefs" on the Tea Party website are the following tenets: "Gun ownership is sacred" and "Special interests must be eliminated." The gun lobby is apparently not a special interest!

The protestors in the streets of the Middle East have not been confused. Beside jobs and dignity, they were out for liberty and democracy—the freedom to elect their leaders. Yet this is what the occupiers of the streets of America were rejecting: the liberty of the 1 percent, a democracy of legal corruption, the freedom of free enterprises. The protestors of Egypt got to elect their leaders, all right: in came the Muslim Brotherhood. Welcome to twenty-first-century democracy!

So back they went into the streets, this time clearer on what they didn't want than what they did. The army removed the Brotherhood, with consequences that now appear to be dire. I hope that well-meaning Egyptians will figure out how to resolve this mess, because many of us in Canada right now have the same concern: how to get a government that integrates our legitimate needs instead of favoring narrow interests.

Some pundits in the West who were quick to understand the early protests in the Middle East pronounced themselves confused by the protests closer to home. "Got a gripe? Welcome to the cause" headlined the *International Herald Tribune* (Lacey 2011). Yes, the gripes have varied—unemployment, income disparities, banker bonuses, global warming. But what has been behind most of these protests—east and west, north and south, left and right— should be obvious to anyone who cares to get the point: people have had it with social imbalance.

So no, thank you, to a compromised center as well as to the pendulum politics of left and right, both of which buttress imbalance. We need to change our concept of the political world.

Public, Private, and Plural Sectors

Centuries of debate over left versus right have given the impression that society has only two consequential sectors: the public and the private. In fact, there are three, and the other one may be the most consequential today, because it can be key to restoring balance in society.

Fold down the ends of the political line into the circle shown in the accompanying figure. This perspective can take us past two-sided politics, to a three-sector society, representing governments, businesses, and communities. **Strength in all three sectors is necessary for a society to be balanced. Imagine them as the sturdy legs of a stool—or pillars, if you wish—on which a healthy society has to be supported: a public sector of political forces rooted in respected governments, a private sector of economic forces based on responsible businesses, and a plural sector of social forces manifested in robust communities** (Korten 1995; Marshall 2011: Chapter 20).

The public and private sectors are shown to the left and right of the upper part of the circle because their institutions function mostly in hierarchies of authority, off the ground. The plural sector is shown at the bottom because its associations tend to be rooted on the ground; we may all get services from public and private sector intuitions, but all of us *are* the plural sector.

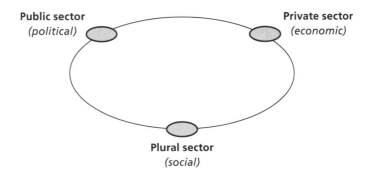

Public sector
(political)

Private sector
(economic)

Plural sector
(social)

To put this in another way, **a democratic society balances individual, collective, and communal needs, attending to each adequately but none excessively.** As individuals in our economies, we require responsible businesses for much of our employment and most of our consumption of goods and services. As citizens of our nations and the world, we require respected governments for many of our protections, physical and institutional (such as policing and regulating). And as members of our groups, we require robust communities for many of our social affiliations, whether practicing a religion or engaging in a community cooperative.

The societies called communist and capitalist have each tried to balance themselves on one leg. It doesn't work. The former has failed to satisfy many of its people's needs for consumption; the latter is failing to satisfy some of its citizens' most basic needs for protection. Trying to balance society on two legs, one public, the other private—as many countries now do— may work better, but it is not working well, because of those politics of compromise. The key to renewal is thus the third leg: **by taking its place alongside the public and private sectors, the plural sector can not only help to maintain balance in society, but also lead the process of rebalancing society that we so desperately require.**

Welcome to the Plural Sector

"If men are to remain civilized or to become so, the art of associating together must grow and improve" (de Tocqueville 1840/2003: 10). Accordingly, let's take a good look at the sector that best encourages this activity.

What's in the Plural Sector?
The answer is suggested in the word itself: a great number of activities. All of them are associations (as de Tocqueville used the term), but only some of them are formal institutions, in the sense of being legally incorporated. The latter include cooperatives, nongovernmental organizations (NGOs), unions, religious orders, and many hospitals and universities. Less formal associations include *social movements*, whereby people mass together to protest some practice they find unacceptable; and *social initiatives*, usually started by small groups in communities, to bring about needed changes. Metaphorically speaking, social movements materialize in the streets while social initiatives function on the ground. Both are found in the plural sector because it offers the autonomy needed to

challenge the status quo, with relative freedom from the controls of public sector governments and the expectations of private sector investors.

What can such a variety of activities have in common, to distinguish them from what goes on in the public and private sectors? The answer is ownership: **the plural sector comprises all associations of people that are owned neither by the state nor by private investors. Some are owned by their members; others are owned by no one.**

Cooperatives are owned by their members—for example, the customers of a retail co-op and the workers of an industrial co-op. Each member has a single share that cannot be sold to any other member. Similar ownership can be found in professional associations and kibbutzim.

Few people realize the extent of the cooperative movement. Amul, a dairy cooperative in India, has 3 million members. Mondragon, in the Basque region of Spain, is the world's largest worker cooperative, with 80,000 employees, in businesses that range from supermarkets to machine tool manufacturing. The United States is home to about 30,000 cooperatives, with memberships totaling 350 million, more than the country's entire population.

Owned by no one are many more associations: foundations, clubs, religious orders, think tanks, activist NGOs such as Greenpeace, and service NGOs such as the Red Cross. Almost all the hospitals in Canada fall into this category: they may be funded by government but they are not owned by government. In the United States, the figure is about 70 percent. Called "voluntary," these hospitals may be supported by donors but are not owned by them, or anybody else. Included here are most of the country's renowned hospitals; the majority of the country's most renowned universities are likewise owned by no one. (By the way, one of them, the University of Chicago, has been the plural sector home of many of the economists who have promoted the supremacy of the private sector most aggressively. If capitalism is so good for everyone else, how come it has not been good enough for these economists?)

Gaining attention these days is the *social economy*, comprising plural sector associations that engage in trade. Cooperatives are obvious examples—they are businesses, even if member owned—but so, too, are many non-owned associations, such as Red Cross chapters that sell swimming lessons.

By virtue of being owned by their members or by no one, plural sector associations can be more egalitarian and flexible, and so typically less formally structured, than comparable businesses and government departments. Indeed, many of the activities in this sector are hardly structured at all. Think of a community that self-organizes to deal with a natural disaster or a group of friends who get together to stop some environmental threat. In fact, this is how Greenpeace got its start. A couple of people sitting in a living room in Vancouver got a call from a newspaper reporter asking about the environment movement, and one of them blurted out that they were going to challenge a weapons test off the Alaska coast. They raised some money at a concert, bought an old fishing boat, named it *Greenpeace*, and headed out. The photo of this little boat in front of the gigantic hull of that carrier became iconic in this renowned institution.

The Obscurity of the Plural Sector
Despite this variety of activities, with so many of us involved in them and many of them so prominent, **it is remarkable how obscure the plural sector itself is.** Having been ignored in those great debates over left versus right has obviously not helped.[12] Activities in the plural sector range

across that whole political spectrum; it is no middle ground between left and right, but as different from the public and private sectors as they are from each other.

Over many years, we have seen a good deal of nationalization and privatization, as institutions have been shifted back and forth between the public and private sectors. Where has the plural been in all this, which can sometimes be a better fit for organizations that don't quite suit the other two? Likewise, there is much talk these days about PPPs, meaning partnerships between public and private institutions. How about the institutions of the plural sector? Great debates have also raged over the provision of health care services in markets, for the sake of choice, or else by governments, for the sake of equality. How about the plural sector, for the sake of quality?[13] Think of the hospitals you admire most. Are they public? Or private?

Why Call It "Plural"?

Labels matter. Another reason for the obscurity of this sector is the set of unfortunate labels by which it has been identified. These include (1) the "third sector," as if it is third-rate, an afterthought; (2) the home of "not-for-profit" organizations, even though governments are not-for-profit, too, and of NGOs, even though businesses are also nongovernmental; (3) the "voluntary sector," as if this were a place of casual employment; and (4) "civil society," the oldest yet most confusing label, hardly descriptive in and of itself (in contrast to *uncivil* society?).[14] Recently I attended a meeting of scholars dedicated to this sector and heard most of these labels mentioned in the course of an hour. If the experts can't get their vocabulary straight, how are the rest of us to take this sector seriously?

I propose the word *plural* because of the variety of associations in this sector as well as the plurality of their membership and ownership.[15] Not incidental is that the word starts with a *p*: when I have introduced it in discussion groups, *plural* has entered the conversations naturally alongside *public* and *private*.[16]

Common Property in the Plural Sector

The plural sector is distinguished not only by its unique forms of ownership but also by a form of property particular to itself.

For centuries, property has been seen as absolute, based on some sort of natural law, even God-given—whether it was obtained by hard work, purchase, manipulation, or inheritance. Today the business corporation is seen as the property of shareholders, even those who are day traders, while employees who devote their working lives to the company are excluded. Marjorie Kelly (2001) has likened this to the ownership of land in feudal times.[17]

The fact is that property "rights" have always been established by human actions, whether according to the law of the jungle or the laws of the state, these usually written by people with considerable property of their own.[18] **Communism taught us that a society with hardly any private property cannot function effectively. Capitalism is teaching us that a society with hardly anything but private property is not much better.**

Now we hear a great deal about "intellectual property": if you have an idea, patent it, in order to "monetize" it, even if your claim is dubious. Some pharmaceutical companies, for example, have been able to patent herbal medicines that had been serving people in traditional cultures for centuries.

Benjamin Franklin had another idea: he refused to patent what became his famous stove, commenting, "We should be glad of an opportunity to serve others by any innovation of ours." Jonas Salk concurred: "Who owns my polio vaccine? The people. Can you patent the sun?"[19] Think of all the children who have benefitted from not having to bear the burden of that market.

Franklin and Salk engaged in a role we call "social entrepreneur." Were they foolish to forego all that money? Maybe the foolish ones are those who have to accumulate money relentlessly in order to keep score. "The determination to do something because it is the right thing to do, not because we are told to do it by governments or enticed to do it by the market, is what makes associational life a force for good, [and] provides fuel for change" (Edwards 2004: 111).

If this stove and vaccine were not registered as private property, and if they were not public property owned by the state, what were they? The answer is *common property.* It used to be quite common before it disappeared from public perception.[20] The Boston Common, for example, now a prominent park, was once the place where the landless could graze their cows. A sign at its entrance makes no mention of that origin.

Common property is associated with the plural sector in that it is communal and shared but not owned: it is held by people "jointly and together rather than separately and apart" (Rowe 2008: 2; see also Ostrom 1990 and Ostrom et al. 1999). Think of the air we breathe—try to own that—or the water that some farmers share for irrigation. Now we are seeing a resurgence of common property in interesting ways, most evidently in open-source systems such as Linux and Wikipedia, non-owned associations whose users create and share the contents.

Today [the common property] model is reappearing in many precincts of the economy at large—from the revival of traditional main streets, public spaces, and community gardens to the resistance to the corporate enclosure of university research and the genetic substrate of material life. (Rowe 2008: 139)

So the commons is making a comeback. Good thing, because it can allow common knowledge to replace the patent nonsense associated with much of that "intellectual property." Believe in common property—replace the market lens of economics with the community lens of anthropology—and you will see it all over the place.[21]

Communityship Alongside Ownership, Leadership, and Citizenship

We need a new word to take its place alongside the collective *citizenship* of the public sector and the individual *ownership* in the private sector as well as the personal *leadership* that is emphasized in both these sectors. *Communityship* designates how people pull together to function in collaborative relationships. Between each of us as individuals and all of us in society is the communal nature of our groups: we are social beings who need to identify, to belong. Think of our clubs and so many of our other informal affiliations in the plural sector.

On the formal side, **organizations, in all the sectors, function best as communities of human beings, not collections of human resources.** But the associations of the plural sector have a special advantage in this regard. With their people free of pressures to maximize "value" for shareholders they never met or to submit to the controls so prevalent in government departments, they can function like members with a purpose more than employees in a job. And with the egalitarian nature of many plural sector organizations as well as associations, these people are inclined to be naturally engaged—they don't have to be formally "empowered." Think here of volunteer firefighters and hospital nurses as well as protesters in mass movements. "At its best, civil society is the story of ordinary people living extraordinary lives through their relationships with each other" (Edwards 2004: 112). Imagine a society made up of such organizations, across all the sectors.

Losing Their Way

Of course, there are those plural sector organizations that fail to take advantage of this potential. Forced by their board or "CEO" to adopt unsuitable business practices, or driven by their funders to apply overly centralized controls, they lose their way.[22]

These days the fashionable practices of big business are considered to be the "one best way" to manage everything: grow relentlessly, measure obsessively, plan strategically, and call the boss "CEO" so that he or she can lead heroically, while being paid obscenely. So much for communityship. Many of these practices have become dysfunctional for business itself, let alone for the plural and public sector organizations that imitate them.[23]

The problem with leadership is that it's all about the individual. Use the word and you are singling out one person from the rest, no matter how determined he or she may be to engage them all. Sure, an individual can make a difference. But how often these days is that for the worse? The more we obsess about leadership, the less of it we seem to be getting, alongside more narcissism.[24] **So let's make room for collaborative communityship in the space between individual leadership and collective citizenship.**

The Fall (and Rise?) of the Plural Sector

Two centuries ago Alexis de Tocqueville characterized the United States as replete with community associations.[25] Intent on limiting the power of government, the people of America preferred to organize for themselves, in plural sector associations alongside private sector businesses.

More recently, however, Robert Putnam (1995, 2000) has written about the demise of the former, under the metaphor "bowling alone"—the isolation of the individual Why has there been a steady "erosion of the community institutions that we all depend on," such as schools, libraries, and parks? (Collins 2012: 8). One explanation has certainly been the increasing dominance of the private sector. But no less significant have been forces of both a political and a technological nature.

Besieged from Left and Right

It is evident that the domination of communism in some countries debilitated their private sectors while the domination of capitalism in some others has been overwhelming their public sectors. Less evident is that both systems have relentlessly undermined the plural sector. To achieve balance in society, we need to understand why.

Communist governments have never been great fans of community associations (as remains evident in China), for good reason: the independence of these associations is a threat to their omnipotence.[26] "A despot easily forgives his subjects for not loving him, provided they do not love one another" (de Tocqueville 1840/2003: 102).

But despots are not alone in this marginalization of the plural sector: many elected governments have also been hard on community associations, sometimes for no other reason than the convenience of their administrations—for example, by forcing mergers of community hospitals into regional ones and amalgamations of small towns into bigger cities. **Community figures hardly at all in a prevailing dogma that favors economic scale, no matter what the social consequences.**

For much the same reason, many big corporations are not great fans of local community associations. Consider how Walmart has blocked efforts to unionize its stores, likewise that global fast-food chains have hardly been promoters of local cuisines, or global clothing retailers of local dress. **There is a homogenizing imperative in globalization that is antithetical to the distinctiveness of communities. As a consequence, while private sectors have been expanding globally, plural sectors have been withering locally.**[27]

Undermined by New Technologies

Perhaps even more detrimental to the plural sector is that **a succession of new technologies—from the automobile and the telephone to the computer and the Internet—have reinforced the isolation of the individual to the detriment of social engagement.**

Consider the automobile: wrap its sheets of metal around many of us and out comes road rage. Have you ever experienced sidewalk rage, let alone been tailgated by someone walking behind you on a sidewalk (unless, of course, that person was texting on a mobile phone)?

Thanks to automobile technology, many local communities have become urban agglomerations where people hardly know each other. "Market" used to designate the place where people congregated to talk as well as to shop—it was the heart and soul of the community. Today the word *market* mostly designates the opposite: places that are coldly impersonal, whether the stock market or the shopping mall.

Electronic devices, the new technologies of our age, are hardy better: they put our fingers in touch, at least with a keyboard or a screen, while the rest of us sits there, often for hours, typing and shopping alone. No time even for bowling.

The social media—Facebook, LinkedIn, Twitter—certainly connect us to whoever is on the other end. But don't confuse networks with communities. (If you do, try to get your Facebook "friends" to help paint your house, let alone rebuild your barn.)[28] These technologies are extending our social networks in amazing ways, but often at the expense of our personal relationships. Many people are so busy texting and tweeting that they barely have time for meeting and reading. Where is the technology for meaning?[29]

In his *New York Times* column, Thomas Friedman (2012) reported asking an Egyptian friend about the protest movements in that country: "Facebook really helped people to communicate, but not to collaborate," he replied. Friedman added that "at their worst, [social media] can become addictive substitutes for real action." That is why, **although the larger social movements, by facilitating communication, may raise consciousness about the need for renewal, it is usually smaller social initiatives, developed in collaborative community groups, that figure out how to do the actual renewing.**

Is the plural sector making a comeback? A *New York Times* article indicated that American "nonprofits have been growing at a breakneck pace" (Bernasek 2014), perhaps partly because governments have not been able to accommodate the full measure of our social needs. Likewise, as just noted, the new social media are proliferating. By facilitating connections among people, they help those with common cause to find each other, even in the same city, let alone across the globe. By so connecting with each other, community groups can carry their initiatives into broader movements.

Will these developments compensate for the debilitating effects that the new technologies have had on traditional forms of associating? We can't tell yet, but let's hope so. Hence, once again, please welcome the plural sector. But be careful.

Beyond Crude, Crass, and Closed

The benefits of the plural sector should now be evident—I hope as evident as those of the private and public sectors. But this sector is no more a holy grail than are the other two. We have had more than enough dogma from communism and capitalism, thank you. **The plural sector is not a "third way" between the other two sectors but, to repeat what needs repeating, one of three ways required in a balanced society.**

Each sector suffers from a potentially fatal flaw. **Governments can be crude. Markets can be crass. And communities can be closed**—at the limit, xenophobic. Concerning "crude," I heard the story about a sixty-year-old having to show proof of age in order to buy a bottle of liquor at Chicago's O'Hare Airport. After all, when it comes to the laws of the state, doesn't everyone have to be treated equally? At airport security, every time a terrorist gets a new idea, governments impose some new humiliation. As for "crass," in 2012 Air Canada advertised a seat sale: Montreal to London, return, for $274. What a bargain—leaving aside the "taxes, fees, charges, and surcharges," which raised the total to $916. (A CNN.com report [Macguire 2012] referred to this as "common industry practice." That's the point.) And "closed" can be experienced by attending a sermon of some priest, pastor, imam, or rabbi who exhorts people to remain loyal to the faith without explaining why.

These examples may be mundane. Far worse things happen when one sector dominates a society. Under Eastern European communism, the crudeness of the public sector was overwhelming. And with so much predatory capitalism about, we live in societies that are increasingly crass. "*Caveat emptor*"—let the buyer beware—even if that be a child watching advertisements on television. "Charge what the market will bear," even if sick people have to die for want of available medicines. What kind of a society tolerates such things?

In the plural sector, populism seems to be its most evident political manifestation, since its roots usually lie in mass movements outside the established institutions of government and business. A populist government can apply its power inclusively, to serve much of the population, or else exclusively, for the benefit of its own adherents (as we shall discuss later). When the latter becomes oppressive, populism can turn into fascism, as it did in Nazi Germany.

Crudeness, crassness, and closed-ness are countered when each sector takes its appropriate place in society, cooperating with the other two while helping to keep both—and their institutions—in check. I am delighted to get many of my goods and services from the private sector and much of my protection and infrastructure (law enforcement, highways, and so on) from the public sector. And I generally look to the plural sector for the best of my professional services—higher education, hospital care—even when they are funded by the public sector and supplied by the private sector.

We just have to be careful not to mix these sectors up, by allowing the dogma of the day to carry activities away from the sector where they function most appropriately. I no more want a private company patrolling my streets than I want a government department growing my cucumbers. And please keep the politicians and the businesspeople at arm's length from the education of our children, without allowing some people of the plural sector to restrict its use for their own narrow advantage.

Is a Balanced Society Even Possible?

Are we hardwired to favor privilege, where power has to concentrate in a few hands—some inevitable 1 percent? History bears witness to a steady parade of this: lords and peasants, commissars and proletarians, shareholders and workers. On and on it has gone, unstoppable for millennia, to our own day. "Stockholders claim wealth they do little to create, much as nobles claimed privilege they did not earn" (Kelly 2001: 29).

Perfect balance is unattainable: some people will always end up on top. Why not, if they have earned it, by protecting people from threats, inventing a new practice, or creating substantial employment? But what if they have come to power through underhanded manipulation, or retained their power for too long, or inherited it for no better reason than birth? Too many people in powerful positions have engaged in reckless wars, built themselves extravagant monuments at the expense of others, or bullied their employees.

In government, there used to be no way to throw the scoundrels out, short of assassination, coup d'état, or civil war. Then along came democracy, circa 1776. With the sovereigns and the aristocrats gone came a new way to throw the scoundrels out, or at least restrain their shenanigans. All men created equal had a say in who led them. Democracy hardly ended privilege, however—that begins with how we are nourished in the womb and never stops. But at least all those men, and later women, gained a shot at getting to the top themselves. This became the great American dream, known as "social mobility."

Of course, things were never totally like that in America. But they came close enough to sustain the myth. And this democracy circa 1776 helped produce the most remarkable period of growth in human history, socially and politically as well as economically—two hundred years' worth, from 1789 to 1989.

Fast-forward to today and have another look at that social mobility. A 2010 report from the Organisation for Economic Co-operation and Development put the Nordic countries plus Australia, Canada, Germany, and Spain ahead of the United States. For example, a son's advantage in having a higher-earning father was 47 percent in the United States, 19 percent in Canada. "Your [American] parents' income correlates more closely with your chance of finishing college than your SAT scores do—class matters more than how you do in class" (Freeland 2012; see also the discussion at the end of the appendix of "Democracy in America—Twenty-five Years Later").

So the expectations raised high by the American dream now go increasingly unmet, although the myth of social mobility carries on. Success stories do appear; it's just that the odds have changed, and the losers are the prime casualties of the escalating exploitation.

Much of the world has rid itself of insane emperors, bloodthirsty conquerors, and voracious colonizers (although shades of all three are appearing again). But not greedy acquirers—quite the contrary. Every country has its scoundrels, but now many of them are outside government, albeit manipulating within it. Short of catching them engaging in criminal activity—and sometimes even then—there is no way to get rid of these scoundrels.

Of course, competitive markets are supposed to take care of such behavior: fail to serve your customers properly, and you will be replaced by whoever does. This sounds good, were it not for those markets of entitlement that favor the already privileged. Elected officials, who should be putting the scoundrels in jail, instead cater to them, to keep those political donations coming.

Nearly two hundred years ago, de Tocqueville asked, "Can it be believed that the democracy which has overthrown the feudal system and vanquished kings will retreat before tradesmen and capitalists?" (1840/2003: 6). Now he has his answer: yes.

Must this remain the answer? Let's hope not. In fact, the U.S. Constitution offers us a way to think about this. Its famous checks and balances, as noted, have applied thus far only within government. So maybe it's time to apply them beyond government. **Why not complete the American Revolution, in nations and the globe, by establishing renewed checks on dysfunctional activities in the private sector, for the sake of balance across the sectors?**

Of course, such balance does not mean some perfectly stable equilibrium. That would just constitute a new dogma, incapable of renewing itself as society evolves. **Healthy development—social, political, and economic—allows**

power to shift among the sectors according to need, in a dynamic equilibrium that encourages responsiveness without domination. And that brings us to the question of radical renewal.

4

Radical Renewal

WHEN THE LOAD in a washing machine is unbalanced, at high speeds it oscillates out of control. We are living in a high-speed, unbalanced world that is oscillating out of control. This situation has to change, ultimately for the sake of balance, immediately for the sake of survival.

Lofty Ideals and Lowly Deals

These days we are exposed to a great many conferences, books, reports, and learned articles about how to deal with our problems. Have a look at some, and you will find all kinds of ambitious proposals and interesting ideas, embedded in lofty ideals. Some of this is quite sensible; little of it is immediately operational. Then have a look at newspaper articles, watch the media, speak to people on the firing lines. Here you will find stories about all kinds of lowly deals, every one of them fully operational.

Lofty ideals in the air and lowly deals on the ground: this is the world in which we live, and it is getting worse. They remind me of a couple of lines from one of Tom Lehrer's satirical songs, about the war against Franco: "Though he may have won all the battles, we had all the good songs!"

We need good songs. They raise consciousness about our problems, which is where renewal has to begin. As John Adams put it in 1818, what he called the real American Revolution "was effected before the War commenced . . . in the minds and hearts of the people." But then battles have to be won. So the question facing concerned people today is, **How can we bring the lofty ideals to bear on the lowly deals, for the sake of renewal without revolution?**

Many people believe that the answer has to lie in democratically elected governments or else in socially responsible businesses. But not so fast: something fundamental has to change before these established institutions can play leading roles in radical renewal.

Not Governments, Not Now

As discussed earlier, too many governments today are compromised or overwhelmed by the very forces responsible for some of our worst problems. Included among these forces are our own personal demands. Where does the destruction of the planet enter the picture when consumption needs another boost and we voters are clamoring for more of everything (except taxes)?

Moreover, we will need considerable experimentation to learn our way to unprecedented solutions, whereas governments, by their very nature, are "not nimble in the face of complexity" (Brooks 2013b). They have to plan their actions carefully in order to justify them in their legislatures.[30]

Exacerbating this is the limited nature of what we call democracy—a word we use too casually. **Effective democracy balances individual, communal, and collective needs, yet many of our most influential democracies favor individual needs, including those of corporations as legal "persons."** This encourages short-sighted competition whereas **we require far-reaching collaboration—globally as well as nationally.** Global warming, for example, will not be reversed without determined collective action, across individuals, institutions, and nations.[31] Consider these prophetic words about democracy, attributed to Alexander Fraser Tytler more than two hundred years ago (ca. 1810):

> A democracy cannot exist as a permanent form of government; it can only exist until the voters discover that they can vote themselves largesse from the public treasury. From that moment on, the majority always votes for the candidates promising the most benefits from the public treasury with the result that a democracy always collapses over loose fiscal policy, always followed by dictatorship.

Don't Expect Miracles from CSR

As for honest forms of corporate social responsibility, these days known as CSR, I applaud it. But **it is fanciful to believe that the social problems created by some corporations will be resolved by other corporations.** Believe me, green retailing will not make up for greedy polluting any more than corporate social responsibility will compensate for all the corporate social irresponsibility we see around us.[32] The dealings and the lobbying are taking place in the back rooms, not the front offices that issue those CSR pronouncements.

Likewise, let's applaud companies that "do well by doing good," such as installing wind turbines or promoting healthy eating. But let's not pretend that such measures will sweep across the corporate landscape in the form of some win-win wonderland. We cannot allow such hopes to deflect our attention from the fortunes being made out of sheer exploitation. Too many companies are doing well by doing bad, while others are doing fine by sticking to the letter of the law. When he was living in the United States, the Russian novelist Aleksandr Solzhenitsyn (1978) wrote about this letter of the law:

> I have spent all my life under a communist regime and I will tell you that a society without any objective legal scale is a terrible one indeed. But a society with no other scale but the legal one is not quite worthy of man either. A society which is based on the letter of the law and never reaches any higher is taking very scarce advantage of the high level of human possibilities. The letter of the law is too cold and formal to have a beneficial influence on society. (p. B1)

It is also too narrow, leaving the door open for all kinds of legal corruption. Whatever is not outlawed—because government regulators have yet to catch up with it, perhaps because lobbyists have made sure they won't—is acceptable. Businesses may exist to serve economic markets rather than pursue social goals,[33] but they do have to be morally responsible for the social consequences of their actions. And this can begin with lobbying. To any executive who is truly concerned about social responsibility, I say: start by getting your company out of our government. **Claiming that government must not meddle in the affairs of business while business meddles in the affairs of government is a hypocrisy that distorts and degrades our societies.** In any country that wishes to call itself democratic, no citizen, let alone any corporate "person," has a moral right to use private wealth to influence public policies.

Look to Plural Sector Movements and Initiatives

If not governments in the public sector or businesses in the private sector, then what? I believe that **radical renewal will have to begin in the plural sector, on the ground, with its social movements and social initiatives. Here, in communities, is where people have the inclination and the independence to tackle difficult problems head-on.** "What now?" asked former UN secretary general Kofi Annan in 2013, about the repeated failures of the talks on global warming. His answer: "If governments are unwilling to lead when leadership is required, people must. We need a global grassroots movement that tackles climate change and its fallout."

Three aspects of radical renewal are discussed here: *immediate reversals*, to stop destructive practices through social movements and other forms of challenge; *widespread regeneration*, as groups of concerned people engage in social initiatives to establish more constructive practices; and *consequential reforms*, when responsive governments and responsible businesses recognize the need for fundamental changes in structure.

Immediate Reversals

There will be no quick fixes on our way to sustainable balance. In the meantime, we must reverse the most destructive behaviors of the current imbalance before they swamp us, if not by rising waters, then by social turmoil.

For example, how much time do we have to deal with global warming: Fifty years? Ten years? Zero years? This is a dysfunctional question, for two reasons. First, it justifies inaction: if no one can be sure, why should I forego my entitlements now? Second, by asking the question, we assume there is an answer and that we can know it in advance.

In fact, this question has many answers, some of which we know all too well. For those people killed by unprecedented storms, or whose lives have been ruined by callous downsizing, the answer is zero years—it's already too late.[34] For some other people, the answer will be next year or a few years later. But don't expect some big bang midcentury, just many little bangs along the way—moments of truth that prove big for those affected.

Many people will have to join forces with those NGOs that have been struggling for years to check the forces of destruction and exploitation. These NGOs do wonderful things, but the problems are getting worse. Their efforts will have to be supplemented by massive global movements made up of many local movements.

Such efforts will have to be focused, and ingenious, beyond just raising consciousness about problems. What's the use of occupying the front streets while the deals continue in the back rooms? Mahatma Gandhi didn't lead a march against the British occupation of India; he mobilized the people by marching against the British tax on salt.

It is quite striking how simple ingenuity can defeat sheer massiveness. David brought down Goliath with a slingshot; Ralph Nader took the General Motors Corvair off the market with a book (*Unsafe at any Speed*, 1965). In the late 1960s in San Antonio, Texas, people who were fed up with their utility company overpaid their bills by 1¢. That simple cent, multiplied many times over, tied this bureaucracy in knots (Gutierrez 1998). From the local schoolyard to the global marketplace, an unexpected tactic can overthrow a big bully with surprising ease. Hence, **beside just passive resistance is clever resistance, especially when it engages people who would not otherwise get involved**.

Saul Alinsky was a genius at inventing such tactics. In his book *Reveille for Radicals* (1969; see also Alinsky 1971), where he claimed that liberals talk while radicals act—"with hot passion"—he wrote, "The opposition is always stronger than you are and so his own strength must be used against him. . . . [T]he status quo is your best ally if properly goaded and guided" (p. x).

Where are the heirs of Alinsky and Nader today? **We need more than occupation movements; we need slingshot movements, to challenge on three fronts: the practices that are plainly destructive, the entitlements that lie behind these practices, and the dogma used to justify these practices.** Consider a few possibilities:

- As discussed earlier, the current E.U.-U.S. trade talks can be a tipping point toward global imbalance, or a turning point to do away with those shameful courts of arbitration, alongside the excesses of lopsided lobbying. Will concerned Europeans find a way to convey to their negotiators that public democracy is more important than private profiteering?

- Criminal corruption certainly has to be prosecuted more vigorously, but the legal corruption—all that lobbying and litigating, maneuvering and manipulating—is far more insidious. Goldman Sachs is under "a wave of scrutiny [by federal regulators] for its dealings in the commodities markets" (Kocieniewski 2013b). In the market for recycled aluminum, discussed earlier, the company claims to have broken no law. That's the problem. Instead of waiting while governments do nothing, concerned people might send the company one of those 1¢ messages. One powerful signal like this can serve as a wake-up call for many companies. Same thing with executive compensation, which announces that the CEO is several hundred times more important than the workers of the company: some workers might wish to convey to their CEO what they think about this kind of "leadership."

- Surely it's time to challenge the relentless attacks on government: demeaning it, reducing it, and co-opting what's left of it.[35] Years of knee-jerk tax cutting to benefit the rich have driven governments to an overreliance on regressive sales taxes, insensitive service reductions, mindless outsourcing, and detrimental gambling.[36] How about this for a sacrilegious idea: instead of further scrutinizing the public sector for services to shift into the private sector, let's scrutinize the private sector for services that could better be provided by the plural sector.[37]

- Our concepts have to be balanced, too. In particular, economics needs to be put in its place, which is alongside the other social sciences. Each has one or more central concepts to contribute to our great debates—for example, culture and community in anthropology, just like markets in economics. Yet economics has been singled out with a prize known as "Nobel" that is not a Nobel

Prize at all (see note 2 in Chapter 1). Challenging every misuse of this label can remind people that economics has to be brought down to where it belongs.

High on the list of what has to be immediately reversed are many of our personal practices as well. But I'll save that discussion for Chapter 5.

Widespread Regeneration

A truly developed country develops more than just its economy; groups of its citizens develop social initiatives that improve lives, enhance liberties, and protect the environment.

Tap into what is going on around the world today, and you may be amazed at the number and variety of such initiatives already underway. Paul Hawken's (2007) book *Blessed Unrest* describes a "movement" of more than a million associations engaged in them. This movement does not "fit the standard model. It is dispersed, inchoate, and fiercely independent. It has no manifesto or doctrine, no overriding authority to check with. . . . [It is] a massive enterprise undertaken by ordinary citizens everywhere" (pp. 3, 5). The book's 112-page appendix lists hundreds of initiatives, under headings such as "Biodiversity, "Culture," "Education," "Property Rights," and "Religion." Yet, compared with what we need, a million is barely a beginning.

A social initiative can start with just an idea, embedded in a bit of human resourcefulness, coupled with the courage to break away from an unacceptable status quo. Then there has to come a period of focused learning during which all sorts of novel ideas are tested. As Gui Azevedo and I wrote in an article (2012: 10): "Social initiatives . . . seem to be essentially indigenous: they work from the 'inside up,' and out, by people collectively engaged. They are not solving the world's problems so much as their own common ones, later to discover that their own problems *are* the world's problems."[38]

The private sector is, of course, famous for its economic initiatives, including many with constructive social consequences, as in the development of new forms of sustainable energy. Likewise constructive can be partnerships across all the sectors—plural-private and plural-public as well as plural-public-private (PPPPs)[39]—so long as no one "partner" dominates these relationships.[40]

What Hawken called the dispersion of social initiatives may be necessary, to let thousands of flowers bloom. But radical renewal will require that they also organize for "collective impact" (Kania and Kramer 2011)—get their act together to become a consolidated force in countries and across the globe. After all, businesses are dispersed, too, yet they have gained enormous influence by joining forces, locally in their chambers of commerce and globally in their international associations.

To my mind, **the ultimate social initiative has to address this question: how to consolidate the many social initiatives into a mass movement that rebalances this world.** No less surprising than the sheer number of social initiatives is the fact that they are hardly slowing the world's march to imbalance. There remains an enormous divide between all the micro good being done by many people and all the macro destruction taking place for the benefit of a few.

I should add that I have no illusions about all social movements and social initiatives being constructive. The best ones open us up; the worst ones close us down. But at least the former offer a way forward, beyond what we have been getting from many of our established institutions. **Responsible social movements and social initiatives, often carried out in local communities but also networked globally for collective impact, are the greatest hope we have for regaining balance in this troubled world.**[41]

Consequential Reforms

Likewise, I have no illusions about being able to achieve radical renewal without the extensive involvement of governments and businesses. It's just that this involvement will require a reconfigured, rebalanced world. Governments will have to receive clearer messages from their citizens, and businesses will have to drop the objectionable doctrine that they exist for the shareholders alone. Then **the necessary reforms can follow—changes of a more orderly kind that we have every right to expect from our established institutions.** For example:

- If democracy is to function effectively, the legal fiction of corporations as persons will have to be replaced with laws that hold corporations and their people responsible for their actions. This can start with the criminalization of a good deal of what is now legal corruption. Why, for example, should automobile executives and engineers who have done nothing to fix faults that they knew were killing people not be charged with manslaughter? Is such behavior less criminal than breaking into a house and stealing some jewelry? As for the corporations themselves, who says they are "too big to jail," let alone "too big to fail"?[42] We need to face the incongruity of corporations having the rights of persons without the responsibilities. If the church could be separated from the state, surely the state can be separated from the corporation (Hawken 2007: 67).

■ Common property needs to take its place alongside private property, especially to end the excesses associated with "intellectual property." And global businesses need to face the countervailing power of global government, in the recognition that "self-regulation" is an oxymoron.

■ It is time that lobbying be taken out of the back rooms and into the public spaces, where its lopsidedness can be exposed and challenged.[43] Likewise, political advertising by private companies—to influence public policies rather than sell products and services—has to be curtailed along with political donations. Both load the dice of politics in favor of those with the money.

■ The whole structure of the financial services industry requires reconsideration, to eliminate manipulations that profit the few at the expense of the many. Must we continue to tolerate futures markets that can intensify starvation and stock markets whose day trading magnifies oscillations? Taxing some of this activity is long overdue. And surely we have had enough of the short-term practices of so many publicly traded companies at the expense of sustainability—of the environment, their employees, and the economy itself. There are other ways to fund and govern corporate enterprises.[44] Also, between this macro financing of the large enterprises and the growth in micro financing for tiny businesses, how about more attention to middle financing for the business and social enterprises that are creating so much of the new employment?

■ Reforms are necessary in how we keep score. "Growth for the sake of growth is the ideology of the cancer cell," said Edward Paul Abbey. Yet no sooner does economic growth slow down than governments—left, right, and center—urge us to get back to our consumptive habits. How about emphasizing growth in quality instead of quantity, for much of what matters most, such as insightful education, humanized medicine, and healthier eating?[45] Doing so can create employment, too—indeed, often better employment.

With these kinds of reforms, we might expect corporate social responsibility to live up to the expectations of its most ardent proponents. We might also expect responsive public and private institutions to support plural sector social initiatives that have proved their effectiveness locally, with the financing, infrastructure, and specialized talent required to extend their impact around the world.[46]

Toward Balanced Democracy

Democracy is on the move right now, but much of that movement is in the wrong direction. After years of many countries joining the ranks of democratic nations, more recently we have been seeing "a decline in both the number and the quality of democracies (integrity of elections, freedom of the press, etc.)" (Fukuyama 2014). We can contrast examples of this decline in four countries with an example of the opposite in a fifth country.

Exclusion or Inclusion?
In recent years, a strikingly similar phenomenon has been seen in four countries on four different continents. For starters, their people elected governments that pushed more established segments of the population out of power. All these governments were community based—the poor in Venezuela and Thailand, the Muslim Brotherhood in Egypt,

and the Russian-speaking east in Ukraine (or was this one just a battle of business oligarchs lined up behind Russia and the West?). Each of these four governments promptly turned inward, using their power to drive a wedge into their societies—or else driving in deeper a wedge that already existed—by favoring the narrow interests of their own constituents to the exclusion of even some of the voters who had helped get them elected.

In 2002 and again in 2006, Brazil elected populist governments, much as had Venezuela and Thailand. But once in office, these governments took a very different course. They faced more outward, in the spirit of the 2002 campaign for "social inclusion," to try and integrate valid social concerns, instead of allowing certain narrow interests to dominate others.

Some Brazilians might disagree with this interpretation, but at least these governments have been trying to find a better way. Indeed, the populist government subsequently elected in Peru, headed by an ex–army officer who many Peruvians expected to follow the example of Hugo Chavez in Venezuela, appears to be veering closer to what has been happening in Brazil.

The consequences of this have proved to be remarkably different, as well. While Brazil has thrived, and Peru seems to be doing well, the four other countries went into turmoil. Into their streets went liberal and establishment segments of the population, with resulting violence. These people saw the new leadership as anti-democratic, using its power for partisan advantage, whether narrowly for its supporters or corruptly for itself. These supporters, in contrast, saw the protestors as favoring a Western "liberal democracy" that, for them, was hardly liberal or democratic. At the time of this writing, three of these elected governments have been toppled, but the turmoil remains in all four countries, with no clear resolution in sight.

Four countries on four continents, all in conflict, with each side questioning the democratic intentions of the other. Something is afoot here that cannot be denied. **So-called liberal democracy is breaking down while conflict is heating up.** Yet denial remains the order of the day, as the powerful nations of the world line up reflexively behind one side or the other.

While it is anyone's guess where these four countries and many others will end up, one thing is clear: many people are frustrated and feel compelled to vent their anger. But what if they end up venting that anger on themselves? What if their own leadership turns out to be their tormentor? Can anyone solve a problem without having a solution, or with a solution that is part of the problem? Things are on the move, all right, but no one knows where this is headed—except, perhaps, that entitled 1 percent.

Three Ways Backward, One Way Forward?

To summarize, countries today seem to be going backward, to imbalance, in three ways, and perhaps in one way forward, toward balance.

One sector dominates each of the ways backward, shown in the figure on the next page by the lopsided bulges shaded inside the circle. **On the left is *state despotism*, dominated by government in the public sector** (as we have seen under communism as well as in many other regimes). **On the right is *predatory capitalism*, dominated by exploitative enterprises in the private sector** (as we have been discussing here). **And at the bottom is *exclusive populism*, where some segment of the plural sector**

dominates society, excluding even other segments in that sector (as did the Muslim Brotherhood in Egypt). Take your choice—crude, crass, or closed—bearing in mind that one can lead to another. Exclusive populism easily gives rise to state despotism (as in Nazi Germany), while the fall of state despotism in the communist regimes of Eastern Europe has encouraged the growth of predatory capitalism in the West.

Imbalance and Balance

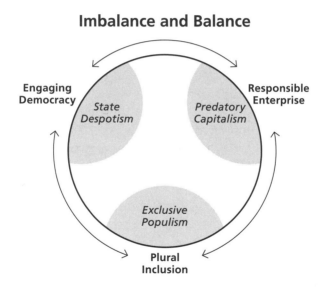

In contrast, **connected around the outside of the circle, in the spirit of balance, are** *plural inclusion*, **based on open collaboration;** *responsible enterprise*, **concerned with the legitimate needs of all stakeholders; and** *engaging democracy*, **which seeks widespread involvement of the citizenry.** No one of these can rebalance society, but together they can.

Francis Fukuyama revisited his "End of History?" article in 2014, on its twenty-fifth anniversary. He looked around and saw only inferior alternatives to that liberal democracy—for example, in China, Russia, and Iran. He might have looked elsewhere. He might also have considered the many people around the world who have difficulty distinguishing liberal democracy from predatory capitalism. Regardless of any perceptions and misperceptions, we cannot continue in the West to sweep such concerns under the rug.

While acknowledging some of the current political turmoil, Fukuyama did not try to explain it so much as dismiss it, as temporary. I hope that he is right but fear that he is wrong (see Mintzberg 2014).

Will so many of us continue to turn inward, allowing some form of domination to drag us down? Or will we break out of this downward spiral, for the sake of a sustainable future? What we have been seeing in parts of South America, also in places such as Germany and Scandinavia, which have retained a certain balance, offers some hope. Can these places serve as examples to restore balance in those countries that have lost it, as well as the ones that never had it?

For this to happen, **we shall have to rethink democracy, to reclaim it from private individualism at the expense of collective citizenship and cultural communityship.** We shall also have to stop that swinging between left and right as well as that paralysis in the political center.

As the saying goes, if you always do as you always did, you will always get what you always got. These days we are getting a good deal of predatory capitalism and state despotism. So **let's try to do what we haven't done, by looking forward socially instead of backward economically.**

Hope Ahead?

We certainly need to get our political structures right, but our future ultimately lies with people who care—about their country more than just themselves, and about the world more than just their country. Let's discuss the hopeful people of two countries, although they really represent such people everywhere.

The "Why Not?" People of Brazil

To quote from a play by George Bernard Shaw, "You see things; and you say 'Why?' But I dream things that never were; and I say 'Why not?'" Hope lies with the "Why not?" people of the world, who keep searching for new and better ways. They can be found in every country, but perhaps nowhere more so than in Brazil.

Brazil has strength in all three sectors: it has proactive and gutsy governments, world-class companies, and social initiatives galore, many partnered across the sectors.[47] The country has its problems, as do many others, not least poverty and corruption.[48] Income disparities are large, but at least they are diminishing, and the economy has seen years of significant growth. Most notably, Brazilians are in the vanguard of addressing many of their problems in ingenious and pragmatic ways.[49] For example, an ethanol initiative brings this alternative fuel to every automobile; there is community participation in the budgeting of many municipalities; the Liberation Theology movement has been carried furthest in Brazil; and, not surprisingly, the World Social Forum started in Brazil, as a counter to the World Economic Forum of Davos.

Particularly indicative is how the country dealt with its HIV/AIDS crisis. While pharmaceutical companies were maneuvering globally to protect their exorbitant pricing, and the World Bank was issuing dire predictions about the spread of the disease in the country, Brazilians were innovating in all kinds of compelling ways. For example, they distributed millions of condoms at Carnival and introduced storylines about living with AIDS in their famous soap operas. As Gui Azevedo, a Brazilian, wrote in the paper we coauthored about the "Why not?" people of Brazil, in place of "any identifiable leader, or general blueprint, was a great deal of creative cooperation," including associations of homosexuals, prostitutes, and hemophiliacs.

Brazil also provides a telling example of what can happen when proactive government is prepared to challenge established global forces, while enlisting the efforts of domestic businesses:

> Unable to convince pharmaceutical multinationals to reduce the price of antiretroviral drugs, and facing American threats of economic sanctions and punitive tariffs, the Brazilian Ministry of Health, supported by a clause in Brazilian industrial property law that limited rights in cases of "national emergency," ordered federal research laboratories to develop the necessary technology and granted "compulsory licenses" to produce the medications locally. Eventually, surprised by the laboratories' success in synthesizing the drugs, major multinational pharmaceutical companies agreed to negotiate royalty rights. When, in 2001, the United States challenged Brazil's compulsory licensing at the WTO, Brazil responded in the United Nations Human Rights Commission, pushing for a vote on AIDS treatment as a human right, which passed with a 52–0 vote, the U.S. being the only country to abstain. (Mintzberg and Azevedo 2012: 901)

In 1990, the World Bank had estimated that in a decade Brazil would have 1,200,000 infections. In 2002, it had fewer than 600,000.

Why has this been happening in Brazil? There may be several reasons, including the country's significant size, its linguistic separation from its neighbors, and the confidence and pluralism of its population. But the main one that Gui and I offered in our article is not about Brazil, but about the "Why not?" attitude of Brazilians—a prime ingredient for creative social change.

Of course, one need not live in a "Why not?" country to be a "Why not?" person. Nor need one be greatly creative to come up with a creative solution. Many a person with an open mind has stumbled across a solution that changed the world, as did Alexander Fleming when he found that mold had killed bacteria in some of his research samples. Why not use that in the human body, he thought, and so he came up with the idea of penicillin. And thanks to the new social media, you don't need to be an astute networker to connect social movements and initiatives around the world.

The "Good Folks" of America

John is a friend and colleague at McGill, in the Faculty of Medicine, an American who sees himself as moderately conservative. For that reason I gave him an earlier version of this document and asked for comments. He provided many and in fact ended up becoming very supportive of what I am doing. Here again was evidence of the blurring of the long-established separations among left, right, and center.[50]

His reaction raised in my mind what I call "the John question": how can I reach people like John who would not likely pick up this book but could be supportive of it if they did?

In a recent e-mail, John addressed the John question. Referring to the pamphlet version he had read as giving "short shrift to the good American people, who . . . are mostly very moral, kind, and generous," despite "being bamboozled by corrupt politicians and fat cats who are ruining the country," John suggested that "a few words to differentiate these good folks from the bad system might make the book even more palatable to John." And make it more balanced, too, which I have tried to do in this revision.

The United States has long been the ultimate land of "Why not?" people, experimenting every which way—in business enterprises of the private sector, to be sure, but also in social initiatives of the plural sector. It's just that the former are now so dominant: the good folks of America, despite some successes, have lost control of their country. Too often the public discourses these days are asking "Why?" instead of exploring "Why not?" The consequence is that the country so renowned for embracing technological change is experiencing a good deal of social gridlock.[51]

Never, however, underestimate the resourcefulness of the American people. They "can always be depended on to do the right thing . . . after exhausting all the alternatives" (a quote attributed to Winston Churchill but never confirmed). Americans have exhausted many alternatives. Will the good folks among them finally take back their country and do more of the right thing? I hope so, for the sake of all of us.

Does that mean these good folks of America will be leading a march toward some new world order? No, not this time, even though Americans will have to be a part of that march. Does that mean the lead will instead have to be taken by the "Why not?" people of Brazil? No again, even if they are providing some compelling examples. Two times no because no one people can do that. Rather, as discussed next, we shall have to rely on two persons.

5

You, Me, and We in This Troubled World

WHEN SOMEONE ASKED ME recently, "How are things?" I blurted out, "Everything's good—for me anyway, if not the world." If you are in the same boat, please don't assume that it will remain afloat. And if you believe "Somebody ought to be doing something about this," then please understand that this somebody had better be you. And me. And us—really *we*, as subjects, not objects. The problems of this world are a lot closer to our own door-steps, and a lot further from resolution, than most of us care to realize.

When Kofi Annan (2013) called for a "global grass-roots movement" to tackle climate change, he meant you and me, every time we take out the garbage or exploit some other convenient externality. "Green thinking cannot be the sole responsibility of a few environmentally minded activists, while the rest of us go on living as if there were no tomorrow," he said. It is not the tar sands that create the pollution, but those of us who drive its consequences, in our cars and our votes.

Let me repeat: **Our world is dangerously out of balance and we require radical renewal. People will have to do it. Not "them." You and me, individually and together.** Not by focusing on what *they* do to *us*, but by recognizing what *we* can do for *ourselves.* And not by having to expend so much energy fighting exploitation as by using our resourcefulness to circumvent that exploitation. **Restoring balance in society will have to be our legacy, if we are to have any legacy at all. The alternative is the end of our history.**

Opening Our Eyes

Look around: At a capable friend who lost a job because her company "downsized" for the sake of some executive bonus, or at another who kept his job in a mercenary workplace and gave in to alcohol or drugs. At a relative who succumbed to the epidemic of cancer, thanks to the toxic environments we tolerate. At the lives of people just outside some gated community in which you may be living, and at your own life for having to so imprison yourself. At the gangs of unemployed youths in our streets who are aping the violence they see in our local movie theaters.[52] At homes not far away that were destroyed by freak weather, likely brought on by global warming. ("Not proved," claim the studies sponsored by industries benefitting from that warming, and echoed by those economists [e.g., Klaus

2008] who say, in effect, "How dare the environment challenge the supremacy of our theory?") One or more of these troubles may be coming our way—not on our TV screens, but in our personal lives.

The angst in today's world is not incidental. Like those nervous dogs before an earthquake, many of us seem to be sensing what we do not yet understand. So in the meantime we carry merrily along. When it comes to the environment, for example, we spend a lot more time pointing the finger at others than considering our own behaviors. My little car hardly pollutes compared to your big car (it still pollutes). Our American coal is "clean" (compared with your Canadian tar sands, I suppose). Our Canadian *oil* sands are responsible for only 0.15 percent of the world's greenhouse gases (so let's target those polluters responsible for 15 percent). Why should *we* in the developing world bother about all this when *you* of the developed world created these problems in the first place? And on and on it goes, ad nauseum, each of us blaming someone else as an excuse for our own inaction.

We Montrealers have reveled in some unusually warm dry summers recently while watching televised clips of great floods destroying other places. Yet every time I go into a restaurant, I have to take a sweater to fight off the air conditioning. Down the garbage chutes of this world go our convenient bundles of externalities—out of sight, out of mind—while financial institutions make more money trading our carbon trash: more markets to correct other markets, instead of just stopping the devastation. Are we prepared to explain to our children the state of the world that we have borrowed from them?

Getting It

It is amazing how few of us, including some of the most concerned, get it about our own behaviors. It's convenient not to get it. After all, if the markets don't get it, why should I? If the tar sands only contribute a fraction of 1 percent, what can I possibly do?

This is the perfect formula for disaster. All we have to do is stay on course, a course we have been on for a long time: each of us for ourselves, each of our institutions and nations for itself. Why not, if greed is good?

People are supposed to cooperate when they have an enemy in common. Well, **we have an enemy in common, and that is our problem: the enemy is us—specifically, our own individuality, self-interest fatefully misunderstood.** It has been said that "each snowflake in an avalanche pleads not guilty" (Stanislaw Lec). We are all guilty—so please, no more pleading.

The Irene Question

Irene is a Canadian finance manager who has worked in the private and plural sectors. In reading the pamphlet version of this book, she had two reactions. First, "I did know what's been going on . . . but not the extent to which it's embedded in the laws that I thought protect us, the companies that 'serve us' and the governments that are powerless to help." Second, "I'd like to do something; I just don't know where to start." I call this "the Irene question": what can I do? It's the question that I am getting all the time now.

One obvious answer is to consider what other people are already doing, to join them or else emulate them.

Another is to take a good look at the needs nearby that have been obscured by our own busyness. And by our own mindset, too: we see what we believe. Once we believe differently, we can see differently, and so act differently. Hence, the best answer I can give to the Irene question is not any particular prescription, but the description that I have already offered here.

I can, however, suggest some guidelines. **The place to start confronting the exploiters of this world is in front of our own mirrors. Now!** We shall have to rebalance ourselves if we are to rebalance our societies. Doing this should make confronting the bigger exploiters easy! They function in all the sectors, and so do we—as consumers, voters, and members, as well as workers. We have a direct line to each and every one of them: we need to use it.

So let's hit that "off" button and press "pause" on those other distractions, so that we can look past our personal entitlements and see what is happening on the ground—down the street, across town, around the world, in the mirror. Then, when the next little indulgence comes along, instead of giving into it, we can do something different—just as simple as putting on a sweater instead of turning up the heat. This is good for the environment and even better for discarding an attitude of business as usual.

From this it may be natural to offer help to an infirm neighbor, and then to join a community group that helps many such people. Next thing we know, we might find ourselves on the street protesting the neglect of such people. Better still, we could be starting an initiative to put a stop to such neglect, locally and then globally. The answers, you see, are all around us.

Living the Decent Life

Those of us who live the good life certainly wish to maintain it. But there are a lot better ways to do that than indulging in more consumption. "You can never get enough of what you don't really need" (attributed to Huston Smith). What a waste of the good life. What a waste of a beautiful planet.

The economically developed world is in dire need of social redevelopment. Many of us who live in it have more wealth than our ancestors could possibly have imagined, yet we have made an awful mess in using it. When do we get to cash in our chips to live the decent life?

And when do we start setting a different example for those people intent on imitating our "development"? **By our casual indulgences, we are perpetuating a massively destructive scenario.** Who are we to say to them, "Sorry, it's too late. This planet can't take any more." We have no choice, therefore, but to set a different example, by cutting back on our own excesses while ceasing to cheer on the hyperexcesses of the superrich as some kind of perverse spectator sport. How about celebrating modesty for a change?

Changing the World Over Again

Margaret Mead is reported to have said, "Never doubt that a small group of thoughtful, committed citizens can change the world. Indeed, it is the only thing that ever has." But changing this world will require a great many such groups, acting alone and together, every day, everywhere.

Will we be wise enough to use our resourcefulness to act anew, before revolution takes us to some worse imbalance?

Are we ready to act on a scale that will be unprecedented, for a planet whose problems are unprecedented?

Tom Paine told the American people in his pamphlet *Common Sense*, "We have it in our power to begin the world over again." Paine was right in 1776. Can we be right again now? Can we afford not to be?

Boiling in Our Own Water

A Rant on the State of Our Imbalance, with Some Suggestions for Change

A WELL-KNOWN ADAGE claims that if you put a frog in hot water, it will jump out, but if you put it in cold water and gradually turn up the heat, the frog will remain until it boils to death. Are we boiling in our own water?

Consider the points of this appendix in their entirety. Many may be familiar, but together they tell the story of a world that is dangerously out of balance. Either we stop this, or it stops us. (A fuller version of what follows can be accessed in the original pamphlet at www.mintzberg .org, on pages 77–106.)

Consumed by Consumption

In today's world, we glorify consumption while we consume ourselves and our planet. "In the past, we had to work in order to produce useful things. Today, we have to consume useless things in order to work" (Sibley 2006).

We "harvest" the fish of the sea, as if we own everything that lives, while chemicals that don't live destroy much that does. Are we in a race to discover whether our collective suicide will come from without—be that pollution, global warming, nuclear holocaust—or from within, thanks to the chemical stews that we ingest, inhale, and absorb?

Corporate Persons and Human Resources

As corporations have become "persons" in the law, persons have become "resources" in the corporations. Are you a human resource? I am a human being.

The U.S. Supreme Court has declared that these corporate persons have the right to free speech. As a consequence, some of them have used their wealth to drown out the free speech of real persons, by weighing in on public issues with massive advertising campaigns. (Go fight the millions spent to promote "clean coal.") Others have initiated frivolous lawsuits (called SLAPPS: strategic lawsuits against public participation) to shut up opponents who cannot afford the legal costs of fighting back. And in 2010 and 2014, the Supreme Court opened the floodgates to the money of these private "persons" in public elections. (See the accompanying box.)

Lies the Lobbyists Tell Us

Lobbying is about free speech. Then why does it take place behind closed doors?

Corporations, as persons in the law, have the right to this free speech. Someone in the United States has brought a suit to have chimpanzees recognized as persons in the law (in order to protect them). Surely chimpanzees have a more legitimate claim to personhood than do corporations.

Lobbying is legal. In a manner of speaking, lobbying may be legal. So is bribing, under the label of political donations, which has opened those backroom doors to lobbying. Corruption, you see, can be legal, too.

Everyone has access to lobbying. "Everyone" includes those who have the money to bribe the politicians, or the power to make their lives miserable, or who can threaten their reelection. While the vast majority of Americans supported the recent legislation to expand background checks for gun buyers, the gun lobby stopped this legislation in the Senate.

Lobbying is about democracy. In fact, lobbying destroys democracy. The self-evident truth today is that those people who get to lobby are more equal than those who don't.

The Corporate Press

Most countries called democratic do not have an independent press so much as a corporate press, beholden to the owners and the advertisers. In the last federal election in Canada, a neoconservative party was elected with less than 40 percent of the popular vote but with the endorsement of every single English-language daily newspaper except one. In Italy, Silvio Berlusconi used his control of much of the Italian press and media to maintain himself as prime minister for almost nine years. Is democracy just something we assert and then ignore?

In the name of competition, some people would like to rid their countries of the only major networks that are not corporate—BBC, PBS, CBC, and others. To restore balance in society, we need more alternate voices in the press and the media, not fewer. The social media are making a start, but only a start.

Numbed by Advertising

Stop for a moment and have a look at the next few advertisements you see. Ask yourself how many of them go beyond informing, to demean basic human values (mixing up diamonds with love, for example) or else to lie outright, by commission ("Not a worry in the world" on a Nairobi billboard about a pension plan) or by omission ("Clean Coal"—did they mean clean*er* coal?).

Caveat emptor—let the buyer beware—even if that buyer is a five-year-old watching television. By 2000, the average child in the United States was watching more than forty thousand TV commercials annually (Dittmann 2004).

Why must parents intent on protecting their children have to fight losing battles with commercial interests?

"Who cares?" you might think, since you hardly notice these advertisements anymore. Think again. Political attack ads, which reduce candidates to caricatures, work all too well, by deflecting attention away from serious issues. They influence some voters while turning others off politics altogether—which may be the best result for the worst politicians.[53]

The Commercialization of Almost Everything

Consider the extent to which our world has become commercial, where everything possible is supposed to be "monetized." Prostitution, as the indiscriminative selling of some precious aspect of self, is rampant in our societies. Wealthy celebrities sell their names to endorse products that mean nothing to them; the Olympic Games are brought to us by sugared drinks and fatty foods; university professors and medical doctors readily accept bribes from pharmaceutical companies.[54] Successful people—artists, writers, chefs—are touted as "brands," while regular people walk around like billboards touting the brands they bought. (Please don't judge me by the watch I wear.)

How about raising ourselves up instead of dragging ourselves down—celebrating celebrities who say no and cheering at sporting events without prompting from PR departments, where the coaches no longer have to dress in business attire.

The Emasculation of Government

In the win-win scenario of communism, the state was supposed to "wither away." Now capitalism is working on it instead—at least for those government departments that do not serve its purposes. Many countries have been relentlessly "privatizing" their public services, as if business is inevitably superior to government.

This I have never quite understood. I held my first full-time job with the state-owned Canadian National, the world's most progressive railroad at the time. Now I am an avid listener of CBC Radio, also state owned and quite remarkable.[55] What I do understand is that the failure of the mindless nationalizations by left-wing governments has not justified the mindless privatizations by right-wing governments.

In the 2012 U.S. presidential election, while private interests spent billions on the campaigns, some state governments did not even have the funds to staff their polling booths. Who can expect decent public services where there is little respect for public service?

Meanwhile, under the banner of the "New Public Management," a euphemism for old corporate practices, public services that cannot be turned into businesses are supposed to pretend that they are businesses: put heroic leaders in charge, reorganize constantly, measure like mad, and reengineer everything in sight.

Most activities are in government *because* they cannot be managed like businesses. How is diplomacy supposed to be so managed? How do you measure what a child learns in a classroom without destroying the quality of the education? A senior British civil servant, when asked why there had been such a profusion of measurement in his ministry, replied, "What else are we to do when we don't understand what's going on?" How about trying to connect, to communicate, even to use judgment? (Remember judgment?)

Because the costs of public services are usually easier to measure than their benefits, politicians can cut those costs with no obvious effect on the benefits. These can take years to show up, and even then, not as numbers so much as in the experiences of the people who suffer the consequences—a child taught by a badly trained teacher, a community that finds itself underpoliced. (See "A Note on That Dirty Word 'Efficiency,'" Mintzberg 1982.)

As a consequence of this New Public Management, many government departments now wander around like amnesiacs, confused about what they are supposed to be. Is there any better way to render government as inept as its critics claim it is? And not only governments: there are hospitals and NGOs that have their CEOs, universities that have their credit ratings, food banks that have their business plans.

Globalization for the Global

In the name of globalization, many large enterprises run freely around the globe, cheered on by the powerful international agencies that should be regulating them, all of these economic: the International *Monetary* Fund, the World *Bank*, the World *Trade* Organization (WTO).[56] Here is where the economic dogma has dug itself in most deeply, for the benefit of corporate entitlements worldwide.[57]

When the European Union restricted the use of genetically modified foods in response to widespread citizen concerns about their effects on health, Argentina, Canada, and the United States mounted a formal challenge at the WTO—which ruled the ban illegal. Why the World *Trade*

Organization? Where in the world was the World *Health* Organization? What business do appointed economists have telling elected officials that they cannot legislate on health issues?

Bullying is rampant in the globalization arena. "Level the playing field" is the motto. Sure—so that the New York Giants can take on some high school team from Timbuktu. With the WTO and the IMF as referees. This game is played with Western rules but on Southern turf, except that the rules are promptly suspended when Western interests are threatened.

In the 1930s, we learned that unregulated markets can be dangerous for a domestic economy. It has taken us well into the next century to discover that they can be dangerous for the international economy, too. Yet here we are, sitting around like spectators, waiting for the next economic disaster.

The accompanying box weaves together a number of these points in a story about the activities of one global corporation.

Lose-Lose in the Global Game

In December 1999, I read a Nokia advertisement in a Canadian magazine. It showed the screen of one of its mobile phones, with the inscription "At Revenue Canada your call is important. Please hold." Below the phone were the words "long battery life."

Cute. Would Nokia have found cute an equivalently demeaning advertisement by the Canadian tax agency?

Shortly after, on a weekday morning at 10, I called the Nokia number listed in the ad. In those days, people answered the phone (or didn't). I listened to a "Please hold" voice until a real person answered—after 2 minutes and 55 seconds. Then I called the Revenue Canada number listed in the Montreal phone book. No voice said "Please hold"; a real person answered in 12 seconds.

One example is enough to make the point: why do we tolerate such knee-jerk put-downs of government, in this case by a prominent corporation that did not even have its own act together, at least on that morning?

Later I contacted a friend in Finland, where Nokia was headquartered, with a question: had the company, or its senior management, lobbied for lower taxes in that country? The answer came back as four articles and a speech by or about Jorma Ollila, Nokia's chief executive. He told one newspaper, "High taxation is untenable in the long run," with a thinly veiled threat to move Nokia's headquarters out of the country (*Helsingin Sanomat*, April 27, 2001). "According to Ollila, [the] decision [of the government, to raise corporate taxes by 1 percent,] will cause problems for Finland because many European countries are strongly bringing down their corporate tax percentages."

Ollila claimed that lower taxes could actually give "a growth injection to the whole national economy" (*Helsingin Sanomat*, January 27, 2002) and thereby "create a possibility to finance services of the society" (in a speech to the Finnish Chamber of Commerce, June 4, 2002).

This suggests the following sequence: denying the government such revenue is good because it grows the economy, which in turn provides a base for more taxes, so that the government ends up with more revenue, and thus the citizens in need get better services. Win-win all around. Or is this lie-lie all around—a race to the bottom for the benefit of the rich?

Imagine if other countries followed suit. Indeed, there is no need to imagine. In Canada, when that ad appeared in 1999, the federal corporate tax rate was 28 percent. When I first wrote this piece in January 2012, the Conservative government had just lowered it from 16.5 percent to 15 percent. Three months later, this government was introducing 10 percent budget cuts across much of the federal public service, dismembering many social, regulatory, and environmental programs. The government, you see, was short of money, and this was going to save it $5.2 billion per year.

That 1.5 percent tax cut was going to cost the government $3 billion a year. The cumulative tax cuts since the Conservative Party came to power in 2006, when the rate was 21 percent, were costing the government $13 billion per year (Macdonald and Jackson 2012). In other words, there had been a significant transfer of public services into private profits. Most of the Canadian 99 percent is still waiting to win-win.[58]

So the actual sequence turns out to be closer to this nice little closed loop: put government down, to gain popular support for reducing taxes, which starves public services, so that government appears incompetent after all, thus enabling more of these services to be shifted to the private sector, which reinforces its supremacy. Or to express this point more bluntly: blame the government for not answering the phone so that the government can't answer the phone.

Of course, that ad appeared in Canada while Ollila sought to reduce taxes in Finland. But here is where globalization comes in. He was aware of lower taxes in other countries—that was his justification for lowering taxes in Finland. If the ad did its bit to lower taxes in Canada, then the Ollilas of the global world had more ammunition to lobby for the lowering of taxes in their own countries. This could even have become a never-ending spiral—imagine that.

There is nothing extraordinary about this story, which is precisely what makes it extraordinary. Nokia and Ollila were simply playing the globalization game: divide the sovereign nations to enhance the power of entitled corporations. As a consequence, the planet is warming and societies are boiling so that the rich can get exponentially richer. This we call progress.

Democracy in America—Twenty-five Years Later

Democracy is a dynamic process, not some fixed state. It comprises a variety of components, such as a truly free press, open elections, equal rights, and an independent judiciary. No country can just be declared democratic, as if in some condition of ideal balance. It has to be judged more or less democratic on each of these components, compared with other countries as well as with its own previous performance. The United States wrote the book on democracy as we know it. How has it been doing in the quarter century since the triumph of imbalance?

Not well.

At the start of the republic, all propertied white men were considered equal. Subsequently, with great effort and some awful bloodshed, the rest of the people joined in. Corporate persons joined in, too, without much effort, so that property came back—with a vengeance. Jefferson and Lincoln's worst fears are being realized: self-interest fatefully misunderstood is destroying the republic. "Economic democracy" is not necessarily democratic, any more than is capitalism. Freedom in the marketplace should not be confused with freedom in the ballot box.

Many people in the "developed" world point their fingers at the corruption of politics in some of the poor countries. The difference in America today is that the corruption is legal. Moneyed interests bribe politicians with court-sanctioned donations; corporations spend massive amounts on advertising to skew public opinion on political issues; the extent of lobbying in Congress has turned much of the country's politics into a pork barrel for the already advantaged. As David Brooks wrote in his *New York Times* column (2011a): "Washington is home to a vertiginous tangle of industry associations, activist groups, think tanks and communications shops. These forces have overwhelmed the government that was originally conceived by the founders."[59]

The country's greatest period of development—socially and politically as well as economically—arguably came in the four decades following World War II, when the United States was far better balanced than today. The years since 1989 have borne witness to an alarming reversal on many fronts, including some where the country used to have the best record in the world. Consider the evidence on rates of incarceration (the highest in the world) and obesity (the second-highest); the use of antidepressants (the second-most prescribed drugs in the United States); the costs of health care (the highest in the world by far, with mediocre results[60]); levels of poverty (the highest rates in 52 years of reporting), of voter turnout (114th of all nations), of high school dropouts (18th of the top 24 industrialized nations), of college graduation per capita (16th in the world), even of social mobility (now behind a number of the industrialized countries).

The proportion of American men not working has recently been close to 20 percent, "probably . . . the highest since the Great Depression" (Brooks 2011c).[61] Income disparities have likewise reached levels not seen since that depression, with median household income reaching a level in 2010 last seen in 1996. One poll of working men reported that 70 percent "either hate going to work or have mentally checked out" (Egan 2013).[62] (Detailed evidence on all these points, with source references, can be found on pages 100–104 and 124–127 of the original pamphlet, on www .mintzberg.org.)

If this is what imbalance looks like, it's not a pretty picture. Yet denial remains the order of the day. In revisiting his "end of history" thesis after twenty-five years, Francis Fukuyama (2014) concluded that he was right after all. He acknowledged some of this evidence but then promptly dismissed it as temporary, with the warning not "to get carried away by short-term developments"—to be careful about judging the performance of a political system "in any given decade." It's been twenty-five years. The *New York Times* published an article (Shane 2012) that also discussed some of this evidence, but under a title that indicated another conclusion: "A Rule for U.S. politicians: 'We're No 1!'" In denial, at least.

Especially worrisome is that so much of the American population has passively accepted such myths. What will happen when they have to face the reality? The accompanying box suggests one grim possibility. If this sounds extreme, please read it as a wake-up call.

A Disturbing Parallel

In a pointed essay, Canadian lawyer Paul Bigioni (2005; see also 2006) drew a parallel between some contemporary conditions in the United States and ones that accompanied the rise of German and Italian fascism in the 1930s.

Bigioni noted "the exaltation of big business at the expense of the citizen"; the prior presence of (economically) liberal democracy in both countries, with a concentration of economic power that became political power; the lack of effective anti-trust laws in a time "eerily like our own, insofar as economists and businessmen constantly clamored for self-regulation"; the reduction of taxes on large businesses; "a pander[ing] to the middle class," from which Hitler drew some of his most enthusiastic supporters while he "simultaneously destroy[ed] them"; labor policies that were "a dream come true" for the large industrialists, giving "total control over wages and working conditions to the employer"; in Italy, the abolishment of the inheritance tax and massive subsidies to the country's largest industrial businesses, with the poor having subsidized the wealthy while wages and living standards for the average Italian were dropping precipitously.

Bigioni challenged the assumption that we have enough democracy to protect us: believing this leads to exactly the kind of complacency that allows our systems to be quietly and slowly perverted.

> [F]ascist dictatorship was made possible because of the flawed notion of freedom which held sway during the era of laissez-faire capitalism in the early twentieth century. It was the [economic] liberals of that era who clamored for unfettered personal and economic freedom, no matter what the cost to society. Such untrammeled freedom is not suitable to civilized humans. It is the freedom of the jungle. . . . Such a notion of freedom legitimizes each and every increase in the wealth and power of those who are already powerful, regardless of the misery that will be suffered by others as a result. The use of the state to limit such "freedom" was denounced by the laissez-faire liberals of the early twentieth century.

Bigioni closed his essay with a plea for "balanced and civilized freedom."

Democracy for the Globe?

The American record abroad has been mixed, yet here, too, a powerful myth prevails.

Noble America entered World War II and later brought the far-sighted Marshall Plan to Europe. The country has subsequently promoted democratic elections in many countries. Meanwhile, nasty America has supported its share of oppressive regimes and has worked to undermine some decent ones, much of this to protect the interests of its businesses.[63]

Yet many prominent American commentators, including Tom Friedman and George Soros, see only noble America and so claim that the world needs their country to maintain peace and good government.[64] One of Napoleon's biographers saw him as a visionary because he imagined a lasting peace through a united Europe centuries before the creation of the EU. Somehow the Russians and Prussians didn't see it that way. How many people outside the United States now see it the way Soros and Friedman do?

Must we rely on a single country to lead the world to some just order, especially a country that continues to promote internationally the very model that has been causing so many of its domestic problems?[65] Can the world's most enthusiastic proponent of individualism—for itself as a nation alongside its citizens—be expected to foster the cooperation that the world so desperately needs? Surely this "modern" world can come up with something better than that. Noble America needs to stand up, in recognition that, while the country does not have the answer to the world's problems, it does need to join with other good folks in developing one.

Of course, all the great powers of the world tend to promote their own interests while turning a blind eye to some of the international consequences. But does the fact that this has been going on since the dawn of nationhood justify it in today's world?

The power of five of the world's great nations has been legitimized by permanent membership in the UN Security Council. This has allowed some of them to use their vetoes unashamedly in their own interests. Here is what membership in this august body appears to require: (1) a major arsenal of nuclear weapons, (2) top ranking among the world's exporters of armaments (they are first to fourth and sixth), and (3) a record of colonialism or some other form of international bullying.

We do not need such a council but one that can lead a determined global government to promote the needs of this globe while standing up to the entitlements of economic globalization. Imagine, for example, a Peace Council comprising those democratic nations that have engaged in no war for some decades and have no significant arms exports. Such a grouping of mostly small, nonbelligerent nations could well have greater legitimacy and so be better able to promote international cooperation.

Perhaps this falls outside the box of conventional diplomacy. But so did an international criminal court before that became a reality. We are learning, however slowly. We can learn faster if we keep in mind the words of the French philosopher known as Alain: "All change seems impossible, but once accomplished, it is the state we are no longer in that seems impossible."

In his pamphlet of 1776, Tom Paine wrote, "The cause of America is, in great measure, the cause of all mankind." No longer. The cause of the good folks of this world will have to be, in greater measure, the cause of saving us from ourselves.[66]

References

References in the text

Abbey, E. 1991. *The journey home: Some words in defense of the American West*. New York: Plume.

Alinsky, S. 1969. *Reveille for radicals*. New York: Random House.

Alinsky, S. 1971. *Rules for radicals*. New York: Vintage Books.

American Psychological Association. 2004, February 23. Television advertising leads to unhealthy habits in children, says APA Task Force: Research says that children are unable to critically interpret advertising messages. www.apa.org/news/press/releases/2004/02/children-ads.aspx

Annan, K. 2013, November 25. Climate crisis: Who will act? *New York Times*. www.nytimes.com/2013/11/25/opinion/climate-crisis-who-will-act.html?

Austen, I. 2011, December 12. Canada announces exit from Kyoto climate treaty. *New York Times*. www.nytimes.com/2011/12/13/science/earth/canada-leaving-kyoto-protocol-on-climate-change.html

Bennis, W. 1989. *On becoming a leader*. New York: Basic Books.

Bernasek, A. 2014, March 8. For nonprofits, a bigger share of the economy. *New York Times*. www.nytimes.com/2014/03/09/business/for-nonprofits-a-bigger-share-of-the-economy.html

Bigioni, P. 2005, November 27. Fascism then. Fascism now? *Toronto Star*. www.informationclearinghouse.info/article11155.htm

References

Bigioni, P. 2006, October 29. Power to the people (in suits). *Toronto Star.* www.policyalternatives.ca/publications/monitor/december-2006-power-people-suits

Block, P. 2008. *Community: The structure of belonging.* San Francisco: Berrett-Koehler.

Bollier, D., and J. Rowe. 2011, March 30. The "illth" of nations. *Boston Review.* www.bostonreview.net/jonathan-rowe-david-bollier-economy-commons

Bowley, G. 2013, May 2. The corporate tax game. *New York Times.* www.nytimes.com/2013/05/03/business/shaky-agreements-over-fixing-the-corporate-tax-system.html?

Brooks, D. 2010, September 13. The day after tomorrow. *New York Times.* www.nytimes.com/2010/09/14/opinion/14brooks.html

Brooks, D. 2011a, April 25. The big disconnect. *New York Times.* www.nytimes.com/2011/04/26/opinion/26brooks.html

Brooks, D. 2011b, September 26. The lost decade. *New York Times.* www.nytimes.com/2011/09/27/opinion/brooks-the-lost-decade.html

Brooks, D. 2011c, May 9. The missing fifth. *New York Times.* www.nytimes.com/2011/05/10/opinion/10brooks.html

Brooks, D. 2011d, November 21. The two moons. *New York Times.* www.nytimes.com/2011/11/22/opinion/brooks-the-two-moons.html

Brooks, D. 2011e, June 16. Who is James Johnson? *New York Times.* www.nytimes.com/2011/06/17/opinion/17brooks.html

Brooks, D. 2011f, December 5. The wonky liberal. *New York Times.* www.nytimes.com/2011/12/06/opinion/brooks-the-wonky-liberal.html

Brooks, D. 2013a, January 21. The collective turn. *New York Times.* www.nytimes.com/2013/01/22/opinion/brooks-the-collective-turn.html

Brooks, D. 2013b, December 3. The stem and the flower. *New York Times.* www.nytimes.com/2013/12/03/opinion/brooks-the-stem-and-the-flower.html

Brooks, D. 2014a, May 19. The big debate. *New York Times.* www.nytimes.com/2014/05/20/opinion/brooks-the-big-debate.html

References

Brooks, D. 2014b, April 28. Saving the system. *New York Times*. www.nytimes.com/2014/04/29/opinion/when-wolves-attack.html

Bruce, H. 2012, December 5. Protecting the ozone: 25 years of the Montreal Protocol. *YES! Magazine*. www.yesmagazine.org/issues/what-would-nature-do/protecting-the-ozone-25-years-of-the-montreal-protocol

Carey, J., and A. Barrett. 2001, December 10. Drug prices: What's fair? *Businessweek*. www.businessweek.com/stories/2001-12-09/drug-prices-whats-fair

Chang, H.-J. 2002. *Kicking away the ladder: Development strategy in historical perspective*. London: Anthem Press.

Chomsky, N. 2006. *Failed states: The abuse of power and the assault on democracy*. New York: Metropolitan.

Cohen, R. 2011, July 12. In defense of Murdoch. *New York Times*. www.nytimes.com/2011/07/12/opinion/12iht-edcohen12.html?ref=rogercohen

Collins, C. 2012. *99 to 1: How wealth inequality is wrecking the world and what we can do about it*. San Francisco: Berrett-Koehler.

Collins, L. 2009. The truth about Tytler. www.lorencollins.net/tytler.html

Davis, K., C. Schoen, & K. Stremikis. 2010. *Mirror, mirror on the wall: How the performance of the U.S. health care system compares internationally, 2010 update*. New York: Common-wealth Fund.

de Tocqueville, A. 1840/2003. *Democracy in America*. New York. Penguin Classics.

Dittmann, M. 2004, June. Protecting children from advertising. *American Psychological Association Task Force*, 35, no. 6. www.apa.org/monitor/jun04/protecting.aspx

Drawbaugh, K., and P. Temple-West. 2014, February 25. Many big U.S. corporations pay very little in taxes: Study. www.reuters.com/article/2014/02/26/us-usa-tax-corporate-idUSBREA1P04Q20140226

Economist, The. 2013. *Pocket world in figures—2012 edition*. New York: Author.

References

Editorial Board. 2013, November 2. States take on privacy. *New York Times*. www.nytimes.com/2013/11/03/opinion/sunday/states-take-on-privacy.html

Editorial Board. 2013, November 17. The shame of U.S. health care. *New York Times*. www.nytimes.com/2013/11/18/opinion/the-shame-of-american-health-care.html?

Editorial Board. 2013, December 17. Big Tobacco bullies. *New York Times*. www.nytimes.com/2013/12/16/opinion/big-tobacco-bullies.html?

Eddy, M. 2014, May 26. Amazon strategy raises hackles in Germany. *New York Times*. www.nytimes.com/2014/05/27/business/international/amazon-strategy-raises-hackles-in-germany.html

Edwards, M. 2004. *Civil society*. New York: Polity.

Egan, T. 2013, June 20. Checking out. *New York Times*. http://opinionator.blogs.nytimes.com/2013/06/20/checking-out/?

Eliot, T. S. 1944. Little Gidding. In *Four Quartets*. New York: Harcourt.

Follett, M. P., and G. Pauline. 1995. *Mary Parker Follett—Prophet of management: A celebration of writings from the 1920s*. Boston: Harvard Business School Press.

Freeland, C. 2011, May 5. U.S. needs to cash in on Bin Ladin. *New York Times*. www.nytimes.com/2011/05/06/us/06iht-letter06.html

Freeland, C. 2012, July 5. Even centrists have self-interests. *New York Times*. www.nytimes.com/2012/07/06/us/06iht-letter06.html

Freeland, C. 2013a, March 21. Paychecks tell a tale of unfairness. *New York Times*. www.nytimes.com/2013/03/22/us/22iht-letter22.html?

Freeland, C. 2013b, November 1. Plutocrats vs. populists. *New York Times*. www.nytimes.com/2013/11/03/opinion/sunday/plutocrats-vs-populists.html.

Friedman, M. 1962. *Capitalism and freedom*. Chicago: University of Chicago Press.

Friedman, T. 2009, February 25. Paging Uncle Sam. *New York Times*. www.nytimes.com/2009/02/25/opinion/25friedman.html?

References

Friedman, T. 2012, June 9. Facebook meets bricks-and-mortar politics. *New York Times.* www.nytimes.com/2012/06/10/opinion/sunday/friedman-facebook-meets-brick-and-mortar-politics.html?

Fukuyama, F. 1989. The end of history? *The National Interest,* Summer: 3–18.

Fukuyama, F. 1992. *The end of history and the last man.* New York: Free Press.

Fukuyama, F. 2014, June 6. At the "end of history" still stands democracy. *Wall Street Journal.* online.wsj.com/articles/at-the-end-of-history-still-stands-democracy-1402080661

Garrigues, L. G. 2009, Dec 15. Why is Costa Rica smiling? This Central American country tops the Happy Planet Index. *YES! Magazine.* www.yesmagazine.org/issues/climate-action/why-is-costa-rica-smiling

Giridharadas, A. 2011, September 9. Some of Sarah Palin's ideas cross the political divide. *New York Times.* www.nytimes.com/2011/09/10/us/10iht-currents10.html

Giridharadas, A. 2013, September 22. Draining the life from "community." *New York Times.* www.nytimes.com/2013/09/21/us/draining-the-life-from-community.html

Giridharadas, A. 2014, September 1. From afar, the United States seems at odds with its ideals. *New York Times.* www.nytimes.com/2014/09/02/us/from-afar-the-united-states-seems-at-odds-with-its-ideals.html

Greenpeace. History of Greenpeace. www.greenpeace.org/canada/en/about-us/history/

Grossman, Z. 2012. From Wounded Knee to Libya: A century of U.S. military interventions. http://academic.evergreen.edu/g/grossmaz/interventions.html

Guardian, The. 2013, December 3. Pisa 2012 results: Which country does best at reading, math and science? www.theguardian.com/news/datablog/2013/dec/03/pisa-results-country-best-reading-maths-science

Gutierrez, J. A. 1998. *The making of a Chicano militant: Lessons from Cristal.* Madison: University of Wisconsin Press.

References

Hadjian, A. 2014, February 26. Ukrainian oligarchs stay above the fray and let the crisis play out. *New York Times.* www.ibtimes.com/ ukrainian-oligarchs-stay-above-fray-let-crisis-play-out-1558121

Hakim, D. 2013, October 8. European officials consulted business leaders on trade pact. *New York Times.* www.nytimes .com/2013/10/09/business/international/european-officials-consulted-business-leaders-on-trade-pact-with-us.html

Hakim, D., and E. Lipton. 2013, September 12. U.S.-European trade talks inch ahead amid flurry of corporate wish lists. *New York Times.* www.nytimes.com/2013/09/13/world/europe/corporate-spin-already-on-us-europe-trade-talks.html

Hakim, D., and M. Zurawik. 2013, November 1. In coal belt, Poles spurn Europe on clean energy. *New York Times.* www .nytimes.com/2013/11/01/business/energy-environment/poland-wedded-to-coal-spurns-europe-on-clean-energy.html

Hardin, G. 1968. The tragedy of the commons. *Science,* 162: 1243–1248.

Harris, A. 2013. Goldman Sachs aluminum antitrust suits shipped to NYC. Bloomberg. www.bloomberg.com/news/2013-12-16/ goldman-sachs-aluminum-antitrust-suits-shipped-to-nyc.html3

Harris, A., and M. Cronin Fisk. 2013, August 7. JPMorgan sued with Goldman in aluminum antitrust case. 7. www.bloomberg .com/news/2013-08-07/jpmorgan-sued-with-goldman-in-aluminum-antitrust-case.html

Hawken, P. 2007. *Blessed unrest: How the largest movement in the world came into being, and why no one saw it coming.* New York: Viking Penguin.

Hayek, F. 1944. *The road to serfdom.* Cambridge: Cambridge University Press.

Herzlinger, R. E. 2006. Why innovation in health care is so hard. *Harvard Business Review,* 84, no. 5: 58–66.

Herzlinger, R. E. 2007. *Who killed healthcare?* New York: McGraw-Hill.

Higgins, A. 2012, November 14. Lessons for U.S. from a flood-prone land. *New York Times.* www.ctdebate.org/PDFs/CDA PacketJan13.pdf

Hitchens, C. 1998, August. Bitter medicine. *Vanity Fair.*

References

Jensen, M. C., and W.H. Meckling. 1994. The nature of man. *Journal of Applied Corporate Finance*, 7, no. 2: 4–19 (revised July 1997).

Kania, J., and M. Kramer. 2011. Collective impact. *Stanford Social Innovation Review*. www.ssireview.org/images/articles/2011_WI_Feature_Kania.pdf

Kanter, J. 2009, December 20. An air of frustration for Europe at climate talks. *New York Times*. www.nytimes.com/2009/12/21/world/europe/21scene.html

Kanter, J. 2013a, September 30. Regulations may be snag in U.S.-Europe trade Talks. *New York Times*. www.nytimes.com/2013/10/01/business/international/regulations-seen-as-snag-in-us-europe-trade-talks.html

Kanter, J. 2013b, October 11. European trade chief proposes trans-Atlantic working group. *New York Times*. www.nytimes.com/2013/10/11/business/international/eu-trade-chief-proposes-trans-atlantic-working-group.html

Kaplan, R. S., and D. P. Norton. 1992.The balanced scorecard: Measures that drive performance. www.hbs.edu/faculty/Publication%20Files/10-074.pdf

Kay, J. A. 2003. *The truth about markets: Their genius, their limits, their follies.* Westport, CT: Allen Lane.

Kelly, M. 2001. *The divine right of capital: Dethroning the corporate aristocracy.* San Francisco: Berrett-Koehler.

Klaus, V. 2008. *Blue planet in green shackles: What is endangered: Climate or freedom?* Washington, D.C.: Competitive Enterprise Institute.

Klein, N. 2004, January 8. The year of the fake. *The Nation*. www.thenation.com/article/year-fake#

Kocieniewski, D. 2011a, March 24. G.E.'s strategies let it avoid taxes altogether. *New York Times*. www.nytimes.com/2011/03/25/business/economy/25tax.html?

Kocieniewski, D. 2011b, August 31. Where pay for chiefs outstrips U.S. taxes. *New York Times*. www.nytimes.com/2011/08/31/business/where-pay-for-chief-executives-tops-the-company-tax-burden.html

Kocieniewski, D. 2013a, July 22. Moving piles of aluminum is a bonanza for Wall St. *International Herald Tribune*.

References

(Also: A shuffle of aluminum, but to banks, pure gold, *New York Times,* July 20, 2013, www.nytimes.com/2013/07/21/business/a-shuffle-of-aluminum-but-to-banks-pure-gold.html)

Kocieniewski, D. 2013b, August 12. U.S. subpoenas Goldman in inquiry of aluminum warehouse. *New York Times.* www.nytimes.com/2013/08/13/business/us-subpoenas-goldman-in-inquiry-of-aluminum-warehouses.html

Korten, D. C. 1995. *When corporations rule the world.* West Hartford, CT: Kumarian; San Francisco: Berrett-Koehler.

Krugman, P. 2000, March 6. Unleashing the millennium: After 100 years of trial and error—and some mighty dark days during the '30s and '70s—economic man is free at last. *Fortune.*

Krugman, P. 2013, November 11. The plot against France. *New York Times.* www.nytimes.com/2013/11/11/opinion/krugman-the-plot-against-france.html

Kupchan, C.A. 2012, April 7.America's place in the new world. *New York Times.* www.nytimes.com/2012/04/08/opinion/sunday/americas-place-in-the-new-world.html?

Lacey, M. 2011, October 19. Got a gripe? Welcome to the cause. *International Herald Tribune.*

Lattman, P., and B. Protess. 2013, October 30. Prosecutor moves from anonymity to scourge of banks. *New York Times.* http://dealbook.nytimes.com/2013/10/30/from-anonymity-to-scourge-of-wall-street/

Levitt, T. 1968. Why business always loses. *Harvard Business Review*, 46, no. 2: 81–89.

Lipton, E., and D. Hakim. 2013, October 19. U.S. lobbyists find fortune in Brussels. *New York Times.* www.nytimes.com/2013/10/19/world/europe/lobbying-bonanza-as-firms-try-to-influence-european-union.html

Macdonald, D., and A. Jackson. *What did corporate tax cuts deliver? Background report for Corporate Tax Freedom Day 2012.* www.canadianlabour.ca/sites/default/files/what-did-corporate-tax-cuts-deliver-2012-01-12-en.pdf

Macguire, E. 2012, July 11. "Hidden" airline charges: Dirty tricks or customer choice? CNN. edition.cnn.com/2012/07/10/travel/airline-charges/index.html

References

March, J. G. 1991. Exploration and exploitation in organizational learning. *Organization Science, 2*, no. 1: 71–87.

Marche, S. 2012, May. Is Facebook making us lonely? *The Atlantic.* www.theatlantic.com/magazine/archive/2012/05/is-facebook-making-us-lonely/308930/

Marshall, G., et al. 2011. *The road from empire to eco-democracy.* N.p.: iUniverse.

Milanovic, B. 2011. The London riots and the triumph of neo-liberalism. *HBR Blog Network.* http://blogs.hbr.org/cs/2011/08/the_london_riots_and_the_trium.html

Mintzberg, H. 1982. A note on that dirty word "efficiency." *Interfaces,* 12, no. 5: 101–105. (Also in *Mintzberg on Management: Inside Our Strange World of Organizations*, pp. 330–333. New York: Free Press, 1989.)

Mintzberg, H. 2006. Patent nonsense: Evidence tells of an industry out of social control. *Canadian Medical Association Journal,* 175, no. 4: 374. (Complete version available at www.cmaj.ca/content/175/4/374.full.pdf+html.)

Mintzberg, H. 2006. Developing leaders? Developing countries? *Development in Practice,* 16, no. 1: 4–14. (Also appeared in *Oxford Leadership Journal,* 1, no. 2, 2010.)

Mintzberg, H. 2013. Rebuilding American enterprise. Available at mintzberg.org/enterprise

Mintzberg, H., and G. Azevedo. 2012. Fostering "Why not?" social initiatives—beyond business and governments. *Development in Practice, 22*(7), 895–908.

Monbiot, G. 2013, November 4. This transatlantic trade deal is a full-frontal assault on democracy. *The Guardian.* www.theguardian.com/commentisfree/2013/nov/04/us-trade-deal-full-frontal-assault-on-democracy

Mydans, S. 2009, May 6. Recalculating happiness in a Himalayan kingdom. *Thimphu Journal.* www.nytimes.com/2009/05/07/world/asia/07bhutan.html?

Nace, T. 2003. *Gangs of America: The rise of corporate power and the disabling of democracy.* San Francisco: Berrett-Koehler.

Nader, R. 1965. *Unsafe at any speed.* New York: Grossman.

References

Neamtam, N. 2005, July–August. The social economy: Finding a way between the market and the state. *Policy Options.* www .ssc.wisc.edu/~wright/ERU_files/Neamtan2005_Policy-Options.pdf

New York Times Editorial. 2013, August 31. The hazard of free-trade tobacco. *New York Times.* www.nytimes.com/2013/09/01/opinion/sunday/the-hazard-of-free-trade-tobacco.html

New York Times Editorial. 2013, September 1. Chasing JPMorgan Chase. *New York Times.* www.nytimes.com/2013/09/02/opinion/chasing-jpmorgan-chase.html

Organisation for Economic Co-operation and Development. 2010. A family affair: Social mobility across OECD countries. In *Economic Policy Reforms: Going for Growth* (Chapter 5). Paris: Author. www .oecd.org/tax/public-finance/chapter%205%20gfg%202010 .pdf

Ostrom, E. 1990. *Governing the commons: The evolution of institutions for collective action.* Cambridge: Cambridge University Press.

Ostrom, E., J. Burger, C. B. Field, R. B. Norgaard, and D. Policansky. 1999. Revisiting the commons: Local lessons, global challenges. *Science,* 284, no. 5412: 278.

Paine, T. 1776/1995. *Common sense.* New York: Prometheus Books.

Parra-Bernal, G. 2012, June 12. Lowest Brazil rates unlikely to jump-start Bovespa. http://uk.reuters.com/article/2012/06/12/uk-earnings-brazil-rates-idUKBRE85B0X020120612

Polanyi, K. 1944. *The great transformation: The political and economic origins of our time.* New York: Beacon.

Pollack, A. 2011, July 29. Ruling upholds gene patent in cancer test. *New York Times.* www.nytimes.com/2011/07/30/business/gene-patent-in-cancer-test-upheld-by-appeals-panel.html

Porter, M. E., and E. O. Teisberg. 2004. Redefining competition in health care. *Harvard Business Review,* 82, no. 6: 65–76.

Porter, M. E., and E. O. Teisberg. 2006. *Redefining health care: Creating value-based competition on results.* Watertown, MA: Harvard Business Press.

Protess, B., and P. Lattman. 2013, November 6. Case proves firms are not "too big to jail." *New York Times.* http://dealbook.nytimes .com/2013/11/04/after-a-decade-sac-capital-blinks/

References

Protess, B., and J. Silver-Greenberg. 2013, October 25. JPMorgan is a target in Madoff inquiry. *New York Times*. http://dealbook .nytimes.com/2013/10/23/madoff-action-seen-as-possible-for-jpmorgan/

Putnam, R. D. 1995. Bowling alone: America's declining social capital. *Journal of Democracy,* 6, no. 1: 65–78.

Putnam, R. D. 2000. *Bowling alone: The collapse and revival of American community.* New York: Simon & Schuster.

Putnam, R. D. 2013, August 3. Crumbling American dreams. *New York Times*. opinionator.blogs.nytimes.com/2013/08/03/ crumbling-american-dreams/

Rattner, S. 2013, May 23. The corporate tax dodge. *New York Times*. opinionator.blogs.nytimes.com/2013/05/23/the-corporate-tax-dodge/

Reed, S. 2013, December 17. Global coal use rising, despite climate fears. *International New York Times*. www.elp.com/news/ 2013/12/17/global-coal-use-rising-despite-climate-fears.html

Reich, R. B. 2011. *Aftershock: The next economy and America's future.* New York: Vintage Books.

Robinson, W. I. 2011, January–February. The global capital leviathan. *Radical Philosophy,* 165. www.radicalphilosophy .com/commentary/the-global-capital-leviathan

Rowe, J. 2008. *The parallel economy of the commons.* jonathanrowe .org/the-parallel-economy-of-the-commons

Rowland, W. 2013, June 17. Saving the CBC: Balancing profit and public service. http://fullcomment.nationalpost.com/ 2013/06/17/wade-rowland-a-better-model-for-the-cbc/

Sachs, J. 2011, April 30. The global economy's corporate crime wave. *Project Syndicate*. www.project-syndicate.org/ commentary/the-global-economy-s-corporate-crime-wave

Shane, S. 2012, October 22. A rule for U.S. politicians: "We're No. 1!" Political culture leaves little place for candidates who highlight problems. *International Herald Tribune*. http://iht .newspaperdirect.com/epaper/viewer.aspx

Sharma, R. 2012, May–June. Bearish on Brazil: The commodity slowdown and the end of the magic moment. *Foreign Affairs*.

References

Sibley, A. 2006, February. *Knights of the productivity grail.* http://equilibrium-economicum.net/productivity.htm

Smith, A. 1776. *An inquiry into the nature and causes of the wealth of nations.* State College, PA: Penn State Electronic Classics.

Solzhenitsyn, A. 1978, June 10. Solzhenitsyn at Harvard: Why the West has lost its spirit. *Montreal Star News and Review,* B1.

Sorkin, A. R. 2013, November 13. Profit motive could spur philanthropy. *New York Times.* http://dealbook.nytimes.com/2013/11/11/plan-to-finance-philanthropy-shows-the-power-of-a-simple-question/?

Soros, G. 2004. *The bubble of American supremacy: The costs of Bush's war in Iraq.* New York: Perseus Books.

Stewart, J. B. 2013, November 6. SAC: A textbook case of corporate prosecution. *New York Times.* http://dealbook.nytimes.com/2013/11/04/sac-a-textbook-case-of-corporate-prosecution/

Stiglitz, J. E. 2011, May. Of the 1%, by the 1%, for the 1%. *Vanity Fair.*

Swift, J. 1999. *Civil society in question.* Toronto: Between the Lines.

Tavernise, S. 2013, December 13. Big Tobacco steps up its barrage of litigation. *International New York Times.*

Tytler, A. F. N.d. Lecture on why democracies fail (unverified).

Vossoughi, S. 2011. Is the social sector thinking small enough? *Harvard Business Review,* 89, no. 12.

Wallach, L., and M. Sforza. 1999. *The WTO: Five years of reasons to resist corporate globalization.* New York: Seven Stories Press.

World Economic Forum. 2006, January 28. *Global business— Saviour or scapegoat?* www.weforum.org/sessions/summary/global-business-saviour-or-scapegoat

Zaleznik, A. 1977. Managers and leaders: Are they different? *Harvard Business Review,* 55, no. 3, 67–78.

References

References to the author's publications related to points in the text

On getting the government we deserve

Mintzberg, H. 2010, November 17. Getting the government we deserve, *Huffington Post*. www.huffingtonpost.com/henry-mintzberg/getting-the-government-e_1_b_784781.html.

On the pharmaceutical industry

Mintzberg, H. 2006. Patent nonsense: Evidence tells of an industry out of social control. *Canadian Medical Association Journal*, 175, no. 4: 374. Complete version available at www.cmaj.ca/content/175/4/374.full.pdf+html.)

On plural sector organizations

Mintzberg, H., R. Molz, E. Raufflet, P. Sloan, C. Abdallah, R. Bercuvitz, and C. H. Tzeng. 2005. The invisible world of association. *Leader to Leader*, 2005, no. 36: 37. www.hesselbeininstitute.org/knowledgecenter/journal.aspx?ArticleID=36

On communityship vs leadership

Mintzberg, H. 2006. The leadership debate with Henry Mintzberg: Community-ship is the answer. *FT.com*. www.ft.com/intl/cms/s/2/c917c904-6041-11db-a716-0000779e2340,dwp_uuid=8d70957c-6288-11db-8faa-0000779e2340.html#axzz1nL67BT00

Mintzberg, H. 2009. Rebuilding companies as communities. *Harvard Business Review*, 87, no. 7. hbr.org/2009/07/rebuilding-companies-as-communities/ar/1

On management

Mintzberg, H. 2013. *Simply managing*. San Francisco: Berrett-Koehler and Pearson.

On measurement and efficiency

Mintzberg, H. 1982. A note on that dirty word "efficiency." *Interfaces*, 12, no. 5: 101–105. (Also in *Mintzberg on management: Inside our strange world of organizations*, pp. 330–333. New York: Free Press, 1989.)

References

Mintzberg, H. 2009. The soft underbelly of hard data. In *Managing*, pp. 176–179. San Francisco: Berrett-Koehler.

On corporate social responsibility and the letter of the law

Mintzberg, H. 1983. The case for corporate social responsibility. *Journal of Business Strategy*, 4, no. 2.

Mintzberg, H. 1984. Who should control the corporation? *California Management Review*, 27, no. 1: 90.

Mintzberg, H. 1989. *Mintzberg on management: Inside our strange world of organizations.* Chapters 28, 30, 31. New York: Free Press.

On social initiatives

Mintzberg, H., and G. Azevedo. 2012. Fostering "Why not?" social initiatives—Beyond business and governments. *Development in Practice*, 22, no. 7, 895–908. https://www.mcgill.ca/channels/sites/mcgill.ca.channels/files/channels/attach/27_mintzberg_henry_-_fostering_why_not.pdf

On strategy as emergent learning

Mintzberg, H. 1987. Crafting strategy. *Harvard Business Review*, 65, no.: 66–75. www.hbr.org/search/87407&legacy=true?id=87407

Mintzberg, H. 1994. *The rise and fall of strategic planning.* New York: Free Press.

Mintzberg, H. 2007. *Tracking strategies: Towards a general theory of strategy formation.* Oxford: Oxford University Press.

Mintzberg, H. 2012, August. The lost years? Or finding Japan? *Diamond Harvard Business Review.* (In Japanese; available in English at www.mintzberg.org/sites/default/files/Lost_Years_or_Finding_Japan.pdf.)

Mintzberg, H., B. Ahlstrand, and J. Lampel. 2009. *Strategy safari.* 2nd ed. London: Prentice Hall International.

Mintzberg, H., and J. A. Waters. 1985. Of strategies, deliberate and emergent. *Strategic Management Journal*, 6, no. 3: 257–272.

References

On productivity

Mintzberg, H. 2007. Productivity is killing American enterprise. *Harvard Business Review*, 85, no. 7: 25. www.hbr.org/2007/07/productivity-is-killing-american-enterprise/ar/1

Mintzberg, H. 2011. How the enterprises trashed the economy. *Economist Online.* www.economist.com/blogs/freeexchange/2010/12/management. See also www.mintzberg.org/enterprise

On the MBA

The Economist. 2012. Business education: Would the economy be better off without MBA students? A debate between Henry Mintzberg and Paul Danos. *Economist Debates.* www.economist.com/debate/overview/241

Mintzberg, H. 2004. *Managers not MBAs: A hard look at the soft practice of managing and management development.* San Francisco: Berrett-Koehler.

On the development of managers

Mintzberg, H. 2011. From management development to organization development with IMpact. *OD Practitioner*, 43, no. 3.

Mintzberg, H. 2011, February. Looking forward to development. *Training & Development.*

Mintzberg, H. 2012. Developing naturally: From management to organization to society to selves. In *The handbook for teaching leadership*, ed. S. Snook, N. Nohria, and R. Khurana. Thousand Oaks, CA: Sage.

For programs we have created that enable managers to learn from their own experience, see www.impm.org. (a master's in practicing management), www.imhl.info (for health care managers), and www.CoachingOurselves.com (in the workplace).

On the off button

Mintzberg, H., & Todd, P. 2012. The offline executive. *Strategy +Business*, Winter, no. 69.

References

On the new public management

Mintzberg, H. 1996. Managing government, governing management. *Harvard Business Review*, 74, no. 3: 75. http://hbr.org/search/96306&legacy=true?id=96306

On strategic planning

Mintzberg, H. 1994. *The rise and fall of strategic planning*. New York: Simon & Schuster.

On models of economic development

Mintzberg, H. 2006. Developing leaders? Developing countries? *Development in Practice*, 16, no. 1: 4–14. (Also appeared in *Oxford Leadership Journal*, 1, no. 2, 2010.)

On the Canadian perspective on world issues

Canadians on Balance—a collection with Yvan Allaire and Mihaela Firsirotu (in progress)

On managing health care

Glouberman, S., and H. Mintzberg. 2001. Managing the care of health and the cure of disease. Part I: Differentiation & Part II: Integration. *Health Care Management Review,* 26, no. 1: 56–84.

Mintzberg, H. 2012. Managing the myths of health care. *World Hospitals and Health Services*, 48, no. 3.

Mintzberg, H. (forthcoming monograph). *Managing the myths of health care.*

On management as the problem of the American economy

Mintzberg, H. 2011a. How the enterprises trashed the economy. *Economist Online.* www.economist.com/blogs/freeexchange/2010/12/management.

Mintzberg, H. 2011b. Who will fix the U.S. economy? *Project Syndicate.* www.project-syndicate.org/commentary/mintzberg3/English

Mintzberg, H. 2013. *Rebuilding American enterprise.* www.mintzberg.org/enterprise

References

For a recent response to Fukuyama's revisiting of his "End of History"

Mintzberg, H. 2014, July 11. The end of thinking? *World Post*, www
.huffingtonpost.com/henry-mintzberg/the-end-of-thinking
_b_5575017.html?utm_hp_ref=world&ir+WorldPost

For antecedents to this book

Mintzberg, H. 1992. Learning in (and from) Eastern Europe.
Scandinavian Journal of Management, 8, no. 4: 335–338.

Mintzberg, H. 1996. Managing government, governing management. *Harvard Business Review*, 74, no. 3: 75.

Mintzberg, H. 2002. The economist who never came back.
Scandinavian Journal of Management, 18, no. 4: 616–618.

*For a full list of the author's publications, see www.mintzberg
.org/articles and /books.*

For sources of the U.S. statistics referred to in the appendix

See www.mintzberg.org/sites/default/files/rebalancing_society_
pamphlet.pdf.

Index

Index

Index

Index

Lenin, V., 1
Letter of the law, 50
Liberal democracy, 60, 61, 63, 90
Liberal pluralism, 112n65
Liberation Theology movement in Brazil, 64
Liberties of individuals and corporations, 3
Lincoln, Abraham, 3, 4, 88
LinkedIn, 39
Linux, 34
Lobbying, 9, 13–14, 15, 50, 79
  expenditures on, 110n58
  on gun ownership, 26, 107n51
  and legal corruption, 50, 53, 79
  on privacy legislation, 108n53
  reform of, 58, 104n43
London riots, 107–108n52

Management
  of large companies, problems in, 18
  and leadership, 100n24
  of plural sector organizations, 36, 100n22
  of public services as businesses, 82–83
March, James G., 97n9
Marche, S., 101n29
Market economy, 10–12, 96–97n7
Markets
  competitive, 19

of entitlement, 19–20, 44
Marshall Plan, 91
Marx, Karl, 6, 98n14
Marxism, 7
Massive open online courses for groups, 103n41
Mead, Margaret, 74
Measurement of growth, 58–59
  in Bhutan, 104–105n45
  in Brazil, 106n49
Media, 80
  social, 39–40, 80
Middle East, protest movements in, 26, 27
Milanovic, Branko, 107–108n52
Military-industrial complex, 4
Monbiot, George, 13
Mondragon cooperative, 30
Monopolies, 4
Monroe Doctrine, 111n63
Montreal Protocol (1987), 10
Muslim Brotherhood, 25, 26, 59, 62

Nader, Ralph, 53
Napoleon, 92
National Interest (magazine), 5
Nazi Germany, 41, 62
Networks, compared to communities, 39, 100–101n28
New Deal, 4
New Public Management, 82–83
Newspapers, political endorsements of, 80

Index

Index

Notes

Chapter 1

1. This recognition was not, in fact, discussed, debated, or even decided by the Court so much as assumed. In fact, the passage in question, inserted in the ruling as a headnote, was written by a court reporter, himself the president of a private railroad. Such headnotes were later agreed to have no legal force, but by then the precedent had been established. Nace's book, *Gangs of America: The Rise of Corporate Power and the Disabling of Democracy* (2003), probes into this and related issues, concluding, "In general, Supreme Court decisions have granted new corporate rights with virtually no supporting argument, or alternatively have used a strange medley of rationales." The result has been "a full-fledged legal super-person" (pp. 241, 246).

2. Alfred Nobel was long dead when the Bank of Sweden created "The Sveriges Riksbank Prize in Economic Sciences in Memory of Alfred Nobel." Even if it did not mean it to be confused with the real Nobel Prizes, a sloppy press, hardly discouraged by otherwise proper economists, has done it for them. The homepage of www.Nobelprize.org until recently listed the five "Nobel Prizes," followed by "Prize in Economic Sciences." (It would be interesting to know why this was changed.) Would psychologists have gotten away with this had they created such a prize for themselves?

3. These words have been attributed to the Scotsman Alexander Fraser Tytler (circa 1810). The original source has not been found, although the wording would seem to be his (see Collins 2009). The American Library of Congress cites "Tytler, unverified." But the dispute over the words' origin hardly diminishes the significance of the words themselves.

4. David Brooks, a moderately conservative columnist for the *New York Times*, wrote in 2010, "[T]he American story is not just the story of limited governments; it is the story of limited but energetic governments that used aggressive federal power to promote growth and social mobility." He referred to efforts that regard "every new bit of government action as a step on the road to serfdom" as potentially amounting to "a political tragedy."

5. "The Americans . . . are fond of explaining almost all the actions of their lives by the principle of self-interest rightly understood; they show with complacency how an enlightened regard for themselves constantly prompts them to assist one another and inclines them willingly to sacrifice a portion of their time and property to the welfare of the state" or, later, to "save the rest" (1840/2003: 222, 223). On the next page, however, de Tocqueville added, "[B]ut it remains to be seen how each man will understand his personal interest" (p. 224).

6. In 2009, the great governments of the world got together in Copenhagen. Their accomplishment, according to the British minister for climate and energy (note his title), was to "put numbers on the table" (Kanter 2009). In Durban two years later, the two hundred assembled countries "agreed to begin a long-term process of negotiating a new treaty" (Austen 2011). Then in 2012, Rio +20 was claimed to have produced "an historic agreement, because it is the start of discussion on sustainable development" (CBC, June 22). Later in that year, lest anyone was left who did not get the point, a UN Climate Summit was held in Qatar, the country with the worst environmental footprint on Earth (The Economist, 2013).

7. Concerning laissez-faire and the market economy, Karl Polanyi has written, "However natural it may appear to us to make [the assumption of the market economy], it is unjustified: market economy is an institutional structure which, as we all too easily forget, has been present at no time except our own, and even then it was only partially present. . . . [F]ree markets could never have come into being merely by allowing things to take their course. Just as cotton manufacturers—the leading free trade industry—were created by the help of protective tariffs, export bounties, and indirect wage subsidies, *laissez-faire* itself was enforced by the state. . . . Even free trade and competition required intervention to be workable" (1944: 37, 139, 150).

8. A *New York Times* article (Hakim 2013) revealed that European officials had been "consulting with business leaders on both sides of the Atlantic on how to structure a free-trade pact" before the talks had even begun. "Internal documents obtained by The New York Times offer a window into the extent that European trade negotiators allow big business lobby groups to set the agenda. Among other things, the business community was seeking an active role in writing new regulations."

Chapter 2

9. In a 1991 paper, James G. March contrasted "the exploration of new possibilities" with "the exploitation of old certainties," concluding that the latter may be "effective in the short run but self-destructive in the long run" (p. 7).

10. "[I]ndividualism, at first, only saps the virtues of public life: but in the long run it attacks and destroys all others and is at length absorbed in downright selfishness" (de Tocqueville 1840/2003: 98).

Chapter 3

11. "The neoliberal reforms . . . are not designed to shrink the state . . . but to strengthen state institutions to serve even

more than before the needs of the substantial people" (Chomsky 2006: 218, citing Ocampo).

12. In the United States, "We still have one party that talks the language of government and one that talks the language of the market. We have no party that is comfortable with civil society, no party that understands the ways government and the market can both crush and nurture community, no party with new ideas about how these things might blend together" (Brooks 2013a).

13. Some years ago, an article in *Vanity Fair* (Hitchens 1998) quoted a right-wing activist who had been a vociferous opponent of Hillary Clinton's public sector initiative in health care: "I was the pit bull for the attack out here. . . . But I never imagined that the government would implode and leave the field to the insurance industry and the corporations that got in on the first floor." The author added, "[N]obody voted for [this market-medicine HMO system]; nobody was consulted about it; nobody elected it. Yet it . . . is accountable only to itself and to unforeseeable fluctuations in the stock market." No mention was made of the plural sector.

14. See Swift (1999) on the ups and downs of "civil society." Another, related problem is the lack of any widely recognized author and book associated with this sector. The private sector has Adam Smith and his *Wealth of Nations*—or at least that one paragraph mentioned earlier—reinforced by the writings of Hayek and Friedman. And the public sector, at its extreme, has had Karl Marx and his *Das Kapital*. My nomination for the plural sector is Karl Polanyi and his book *The Great Transformation* (1944), although sections of de Tocqueville's *Democracy in America* (1840/2003) could well take their place alongside the works of Smith and Marx.

15. "[T]he landscape of the third sector is untidy but wonderfully exuberant" (de Oliveira and Tandon, quoted in Edwards 2004: 32). "It promotes pluralism by enabling multiple interests to be represented, different functions to be performed, and a range of capacities to be developed" (p. 32).

16. We could also call this the "social sector," but only if we also called the other sectors political and economic.

17. "[S]tockholders gain omnipotent powers: they can take massive corporations, break them apart, load them with debt, sell them, shut them down, and drive out human beings—while employees and communities remain powerless to stop them. Power of this sort . . . comes down to us from that time when the landed class was the privileged class, by virtue of its wealth in property. To own land, was to be master . . . [the] lords could own serfs, like so much livestock" (Kelly 2001: 41).

18. "Virtually all U.S. senators, and most of the representatives in the House, are members of the top 1 percent [of wealth] in America when they arrive, are kept in office by money from the top 1 percent, and know that if they serve the top 1 percent well they will be rewarded by the top 1 percent when they leave office" (Stiglitz 2011). Could all this be why so many of them vigorously oppose tax increases for wealthy Americans?

19. Maybe not. But one company has managed to patent a couple of our human genes, with the consequence that it has been able to charge more than $3,000 for a breast cancer test (Pollack 2011).

20. Biologist Garritt Hardin published an article in 1968 entitled "The Tragedy of the Commons" that became a kind of tragedy in its own right when economists embraced it to dismiss the viability of common property. However, "eventually Hardin himself had to modify his stance. He acknowledged that the problem is not common ownership per se but rather open access—that is, commons in which there are no social structures or formal rules to govern access and use" (Rowe 2008: 142). Of course, the real tragedies were the exploitative seizures of common property: "Enclosures have appropriately been called a revolution of the rich against the poor. The lords and nobles were upsetting the social order, breaking down ancient law and custom, sometimes by means of violence, often by pressure and intimidation.

They were literally robbing the poor of their share in the common" (Polanyi 1944: 35).

21. In *Governing the Commons*, Ostrom (1990) observed that "neither the state nor the market is uniformly successful in enabling individuals to sustain long-term, productive use of natural resource systems. . . . Both centralization advocates and privatization advocates accept as a central tenet that institutional change must come from outside and be imposed on the individuals affected. . . . Both frequently advocate oversimplified idealized institutions" (pp. 1, 14, 22). Ostrom specified in considerable detail the conditions under which common and other forms of property work most effectively. She also noted that "a competitive market—the epitome of private institutions—is itself a public good" (p. 15).

22. "U.S. Civil Society has moved from 'membership to management' over the last forty years. . . . This is partly because the liberal establishment tends to be divorced from grass roots activism. . . . There has been a worldwide professionalization of the non-profit sector and a gradual distancing of associations from their social base" (Edwards 2004: 35).

23. Now some of the big financial institutions are jumping on the bandwagon of providing stocks and bonds for nonprofits. Goldman Sachs, for example, has a social impact fund, designed to "make the nonprofit world more efficient at fundraising. . . . [If] donors thought about their charity as an investment, literally, it would transform the nonprofit sector" (Sorkin 2013). No doubt!

24. Particularly destructive has been the distinction between leadership and management, with the latter seen as more grand: "doing the right things" instead of "doing things right" (Bennis 1989; see also Zaleznik 1977). Try doing the right things without doing them right. Indeed, try leading without managing: you won't know what's going on. (See my book *Simply Managing*, 2013.)

25. "The political associations that exist in the United States are only a single feature in the midst of the immense assemblage of associations in that country. Americans of all ages, all

conditions, and all dispositions constantly form associations. . . . Whenever at the head of some undertaking you see the government in France, or a man of rank in England, in the United States you will be sure to find an association" (de Tocqueville 1840/2003: 106).

26. The first real crack in Soviet communism arguably came because of two such associations in Poland: the Solidarity Union, which found its opening thanks to the survival in that country of the other association—the Catholic Church.

27. "Western development enterprise has been about separating people from their traditional means of livelihood and breaking down the bonds of security provided by family and community to create dependence on the jobs and products that modern corporations produce" (Korten 1995: 251).

28. In fact, the word *community* has become fashionable to describe what are really networks, as in the "business community" or the "medical community"—"people with common interests [but] not common values, history, or memory." A century or two earlier, the word "seemed to connote a specific group of people, from a particular patch of earth, who knew and judged and kept an eye on one another, who shared habits and history and memories, and could at times be persuaded to act as a whole on behalf of a part" (Giridharadas 2013).

29. See Marche's (2012) article "Is Facebook Making Us Lonely?" March claimed that, thanks largely to ourselves, "we suffer from unprecedented alienation. . . . In a world consumed by ever more novel modes of socializing, we have less and less actual society."

Chapter 4

30. "[G]overnment agencies are geared for stability, not change. Their processes are designed to ensure thoroughness, fairness, and certainty. Something as simple as adding bike lanes in a neighborhood can go through over 40 reviews and committees before the first stripe is painted" (Vossoughi 2011).

31. An interesting article (Higgins 2012) appeared after the 2012 disastrous flooding in New York and New Jersey. It compared the Dutch emphasis on "disaster avoidance" with the American inclination to do "disaster relief." A Dutch authority referred to American attitudes that "make it difficult to mobilize public attention and money to prevent disasters ahead of time."

32. In 1968, the *Harvard Business Review* published an article pointing out that American business fought every single piece of social legislation proposed during the twentieth century, from the child labor laws of the early 1900s on up (Levitt 1968). Has that changed?

33. This point has been promoted from the left as well as the right. On the left: who are they to influence social issues? On the right: who are they to so spend shareholders' money? A counterargument is that doing so will make more money for the shareholders. But does it really pay to be good? (See Mintzberg 1983: Chapters 30 and 31.)

34. At the 2013 UN conference on climate change, held in Poland (which has six of the ten European cities with the highest concentration of particle matter, thanks largely to the burning of coal, and a government that "has been increasingly active in trying to block more aggressive regulations to curb climate change"), we had the pitiful sight of the representative from the Philippines, just after its terrible storm, begging for action. "As if to prove a point, the coal industry . . . scheduled its own climate summit meeting in Warsaw [to run] concurrently with the United Nations conference" (Hakim and Zurawik 2013). The International Energy Agency reported in late 2013 that the global consumption of coal, already a major contributor to global warming, was likely to continue growing at a "relentless pace" through 2018. It has accounted for more than 60 percent of the rise in carbon dioxide emissions since 2000 (Reed 2013).

35. At a party I attended in Virginia a few years ago, I listened to a group of retired military people rail on about how awful government is and how dreadful its taxation, without ever

recognizing that, as government employees, they had been entirely dependent on that taxation for their own incomes.

36. See Robinson (2011) for an interesting view on this point. "The budgetary and fiscal crises that supposedly justify spending cuts and austerity are contrived," made possible by deregulation of the financial industry that encouraged speculation, with the resulting "transfer [of] the burden of the crisis to working and popular classes." The "new speculation frenzy by financial capitalists is now being presented as working people living beyond their means, a convenient smokescreen." Robinson described "the austerity sweeping across Europe" as the "Third-Worldization of the 'First World.'"

37. This could start with some pharmaceutical research. The advances are welcome, but do we need the large, publicly traded companies to get them, and at those prices? Thanks to government-granted but underregulated monopolies, called patents, many pharmaceutical companies have maneuvered themselves into being able to charge "what the market will bear" (*Businessweek*'s use of the term [Carey and Barrett 2001]). What the market will bear, many sick people cannot. The companies claim that they need their profits to support their research. How much? Indeed, if you believe that we need to be beholden to these companies for such research, consider this: three of the greatest pharmaceutical discoveries of all time—penicillin, which led to antibiotics, insulin, and Salk's polio vaccine—all came out of not-for-profit laboratories. Moreover, research in a number of the biggest pharmaceutical companies has been languishing for some years. They have been buying many of their new product ideas from smaller, more vibrant firms, while spending huge amounts on the promotion of them. *Development* of these ideas—testing them to ensure their safety and effectiveness—may require large scale, but that does not justify the economic rents that these companies have been getting. (See my 2006 article "Patent Nonsense.")

38. This point applies to overall economic development, and to development of people, too. In an article entitled "Developing Leaders? Developing Countries?" (2006), I contrasted three models of economic development: outside in, or globalization; top down, or state intervention; and inside up, or indigenous enterprise. No major economy ever developed through the first model (Chang 2002). The evidence is strong that the indigenous model is key to development, especially for a nation's start-up.

39. While the governments of the world were putting those "numbers on the table" at their 2009 global warming conference in Copenhagen, resourceful Danes around the country—in citizen groups, businesses, and government—were engaged in perhaps the world's most ambitious program for developing clean, sustainable energy.

40. This is not to say that there is no blurring on the edges where the sectors meet. Organizations can be plotted all around the circle of our theme diagram—for example, state-owned enterprises in the public sector but on the side of the private one and companies with significant shareholding by employees close to the co-operatives of the plural sector.

41. Colleagues and I are preparing for September 2015 a GROOC—a MOOC (massive open online course) for groups—called "Social Learning for Social Impact" (see https://www.mcgill.ca/desautels/programs/grooc).

42. "There are many critics who will say, 'You can't incarcerate a corporation'" (Stewart 2013). Not true. There is a recent precedent for this, at least concerning part of a corporation: SAC Capital agreed to "plead guilty to all five counts of insider trading violations and pay a record $1.2 billion penalty, becoming the first large Wall Street firm in a generation to confess to criminal conduct. . . . The guilty plea and fine paid by SAC are part of a broader plea deal that will impose a five-year probation on the fund. SAC must also terminate its business of managing money for outside investors" (Protess and Lattman 2013; see also Lattman and Protess 2013). Critics have pointed to another aspect

of "too big to jail": that innocent employees have to suffer for the errors of the executives. But many people elsewhere now suffer for those errors. Anything that can reduce this criminality benefits employees, customers, and society alike. Rights also exceed responsibilities, with employees as well as suppliers and society suffering the consequences, when a parent company can walk away from a bankrupt subsidiary after years of drawing profits out of it.

43. David Brooks (2011f) commented that "President Obama has certainly not shut corporate-types out of the regulatory process. According to data collected by the Center for Progressive Reforms, 62 percent of the people who met with the White House office in charge of reviewing regulations were representatives of industry, while only 16 percent represented activist groups. At these meetings, business representatives outnumbered activists by more than 4 to 1." Brooks, a normally sensible columnist, looked favorably on such business as usual.

44. For example, companies such as Novo Nordisk in Denmark and Tata in India have concentrated their voting shares in family trusts. And Germany, which legislated significant worker representation on the boards of its corporations in 1976, has remained one of the world's great economic success stories.

45. The tiny country of Bhutan has become famous for adopting Gross National Happiness in place of Gross National Product. I visited Bhutan a few years ago and, in discussing this with some of its knowledgeable people, was struck by two things. First, the Bhutanese had no idea how to measure most of this GNH. Second, this inability did not matter because they were behaving true to its precepts. (In the words of a BBC reporter, this had become "a way of life.") Then the international experts descended on Bhutan, to help them measure it. Soon each of the nine dimensions had "its own weighted and un-weighted GNH index . . . analyzed using . . . 72 indicators. . . . Mathematical formulas have even been developed to reduce happiness to its tiniest component

parts" (Mydans 2009). Gross, for sure, but happiness? The problem with techniques such as the "balanced scorecard" (Kaplan and Norton 1992) is that it cannot be balanced because measurement favors economic factors over social ones (see Mintzberg 1982).

46. The danger of doing this earlier—for example, in the provision of seed money for start-up, as foundations sometimes do—is that people in offices who believe they know better—with their measuring and evaluating—can get in the way of people on the ground who have to learn better. But once that learning is more or less completed, people who do know better, about institutionalizing formally what has been arrived at informally, can be key to the widespread diffusion of useful social innovations.

47. Similar strengths in all three sectors, including strong cooperative movements, can be found in a number of smaller countries, such as Costa Rica (Garrigues 2009). As for some larger countries, France has had proactive ("*dirigiste*") governments and an established private sector—with the two sometimes overly inclined to cooperate with each other. This last point is true of China, too, which is otherwise quite different. In a commentary in the *New York Times*, Charles Kupchan (2012) contrasted "democratic capitalism," led by the United States, with "state capitalism," led by China. The former, in our terms, attempts to balance itself on one leg (note that *democracy* is the adjective, *capitalism* is the noun), while the latter tries to do so on two legs: a powerful state reinforced by strong enterprises that know their place, with little room for the plural sector. Economically, such state capitalism seems to be doing well right now, perhaps because it constrains individual liberties. (Autocracy has its advantages.) But will it continue to hold the forces of pluralism in check, which it has sometimes done so crudely? Kupchan suggested that state capitalism will change globalization as we know it, as will another approach that he identified with India and Brazil: "stable, secular democracies that appear to be hewing closely to the Western model." Not quite.

Their public sectors are stronger (he did note that "both nations have embraced a left-wing populism"), while the plural sectors of both seem to be especially vibrant.

48. The protests concerning the high costs of the recent FIFA World Cup event in Brazil may have looked like disorder to many people. But in which other country that has blown so much public money on such an event have the people had the courage to confront these excesses while the event was happening, instead of complaining about it afterward?

49. Yet a number of the analysts of New York and London have been bullying the country, as if to punish its people for electing left-wing governments from 2003. One report cited figures (from Sharma 2012) about Brazil's economic growth from 1980 to 2000 not having been productivity based, while criticizing the Brazilian government for expanding what this analyst saw as an overly generous welfare program. The claim was that while this may have reduced the country's inequality, it came at the expense of economic growth. In fact, the Brazilian economy grew at an average rate of 4.6 percent during Lula's years in office (2003 to 2011), just before this analyst wrote the report. As for productivity, there are two kinds: one that really does do things better, the other that is built on the backs of employees—for example, by engaging in mass firings. (For this unproductive side of productivity, see www.Mintzberg.org/enterprise.) A Reuters report (Parra-Bernal 2012) referred to the country's "heavy-handed economic politics" and mentioned a World Bank "Doing Business" survey that ranked Brazil 126 out of 183. (How about a "Living Life" survey?) We can see this bullying elsewhere, too. In 2013, Standard & Poor's cut France's credit rating, perhaps in response to it having elected a socialist government the year before. As Paul Krugman (2013) put it in one of his columns, France was being punished because it "committed the unforgiveable sin of being fiscally responsible [for example, raising taxes on the wealthy] without inflicting pain on the poor and the unlucky."

50. In a column in the *New York Times,* Anand Giridharadas (2011) mused about whether Sarah Palin's detractors would notice if she said "something intelligent and wise and fresh about the American condition." In a talk, she made "three interlacing points":
    (1) that the United States is now governed by a "permanent political class" drawn from both parties, which is increasingly cut off from the concerns of regular people; (2) that these Republicans and Democrats have allied with big business to mutual advantage to create what she called "corporate crony capitalism"; (3) that the real political divide in the United States may no longer be between friends and foes of big government, but between friends and foes of vast, remote, unaccountable institutions (both public and private). Palin went on to condemn corporate lobbyists, special interests, and "the collusion of big government and big business and big finance to the detriment of all the rest," and to distinguish good from bad capitalists, meaning small ones that take risks from big ones that live off bailouts and dodge taxes, while not creating jobs.
    Was Palin on the left or the right in making these comments, so similar to ones being made here? (See also Freeland 2013a, 2013b.)
51. The country remains unable to rid itself of an anachronistic electoral college or adopt a system of measurement used most everywhere else, let alone stop being bamboozled by its gun lobby. (Do the people of America have the right to bear nuclear arms?) The country has declared wars on poverty, drugs, and more, to no avail.

Chapter 5

52. On the *HBR Blog Network,* Branko Milanovic, the lead economist of the World Bank research group, wrote in the summer of 2011, "The reason [behind the riots in London] lies in inequality of incomes and wealth that the neo-liberal reforms have

produced, combined with an incessant ideological emphasis on material success and consumption as key desirable features of life." He described this as "ideological bludgeoning. . . . [T]he young . . . 'bought' the ideology that wealth equals ethical superiority but found themselves on the wrong side of the equation. The venues that could have led them to wealth were closed—by rising unemployment, cuts in social services, higher costs of education, higher rents, and not least almost open corruption and immorality of the elites. . . . They see the old welfare economies disappearing, while politicians, businessmen, and music stars cynically seize society's riches [and] they don't have an alternative social blueprint. If they truly believed that a different world is possible, they would have organized into political groups, not mobs." Milanovic concluded with the following: "The challenge, should we choose to accept it, is to figure out a way of engaging a generation that doesn't seem to want to be engaged. Ideas welcome."

Appendix

53. As I wrote this section initially, Facebook's entry to the stock market was getting great attention. The question was, How would it use advertising to exploit its enormous database? More important questions could have been, Where would the line be drawn between profit and privacy, and by whom? What we do know is that companies now initially draw those lines in their own interests—the default position seems to be to do what you can until you get caught or stopped. Will the regulators or the courts ever catch up? "In Washington, lobbyists from technology, marketing, and related industries, have effectively put the brakes on privacy legislation" (*New York Times* editorial, November 5, 2013).

54. If my use of the word *prostitution* seems excessive, consider this passage from an article by the Harvard Business School professor who for many years taught its most popular elective course: "George Bernard Shaw, the famous playwright and social thinker, reportedly once claimed that while on

an ocean voyage he met a celebrated actress on deck and asked her whether she would be willing to sleep with him for a million dollars. She was agreeable. He followed with a counterproposal: 'What about ten dollars?' 'What do you think I am?' she responded indignantly. He replied, 'We've already established that—now we're just haggling over price'" (Jensen and Meckling 1994). Instead of qualifying this in any way, Jensen and his colleague followed the story with this statement: "Like it or not, individuals are willing to sacrifice a little of almost anything we care to name, even reputation or morality, for a sufficiently large quantity of other desired things." In other words, a generation of students from the school that has had the greatest influence on corporate behavior was taught that, pushed to the limit, we are all prostitutes.

55. After the CBC dropped radio advertising in 1975, "the result was . . . an explosion of creative excellence that earned to the network a large and fanatically loyal audience" (Rowland 2013).

56. To this list might be added some other international institutions, including the Organisation for *Economic* Co-operation and Development and the World *Economic* Forum, whose 2006 conference in Davos included a session entitled "Global Business: Savior or Scapegoat." Some choice! In that session, one panel member, the chairman of JPMorgan Chase, went on about the few bad apples who were damaging the reputation of big business. On September 1, 2013, after a string of scandals concerning the alleged manipulation of energy markets, criminal investigations of mortgage securities, and the hiring of the children of Chinese political leaders, the *New York Times* published an editorial entitled "Chasing JPMorgan Chase" about its "sheer size, and scope and complexity . . . encourag[ing] speculative and bad behavior." Subsequently, the company agreed to a $13 billion settlement on its mortgage activities (Protess and Silver-Greenberg 2013) and was being sued in connection with the Goldman Sachs aluminum scandal (Harris 2013).

57. An earlier head of WTO was quoted as describing environment-based regulations and standards as "doomed to fail and could only damage the global trading system" (Wallach and Sforza 1999: 28; see also Korten 1995: Chapter 13 on the WTO).

58. The United States has three regimes for income taxes, which may illustrate the imbalance in its society better than anything else. (1) *Full taxation for regular Americans and anyone living elsewhere deemed by the U.S. government to be an American citizen.* The latter are required to file tax returns in the United States, no matter where they live—even if they were registered as citizens by their parents and have never spent a day in the country—and to pay whatever exceeds the taxes they have paid where they do live. (2) *Low taxation for American corporations pretending to live abroad.* The U.S. government is prepared to track down its citizens, but not its corporations. Many have been able to maneuver the presence of their headquarters in countries with low tax rates (Bowley 2013). One study by the Congressional Research Service found that in 2008, subsidiaries of American corporations generated 43 percent of their profits in five prominent tax havens where they had 4 percent of their foreign employment and 7 percent of their foreign investment (Rattner 2013). There can be no more quintessentially American company than General Electric. Almost half of its employees work in the United States, where almost half its revenues are generated. In 2010, GE reported worldwide profits of $14.2 billion, only $5.1 billion of it claimed to have come from operations in the United States. The company paid no U.S. taxes at all that year; in fact, it claimed a tax benefit of $3.2 billion. From 2005 to 2010, the company declared $26 billion in American profits while receiving a net tax *benefit* of $4.1 billion. "In 2010, 25 of the 100 largest U.S. companies paid their CEOs more than they paid in U.S. taxes. . . . Twenty spent more on lobbying and eighteen gave more . . . in bundled contributions to political candidates" (Collins 2012: 3, 53). This activity

did, however, create employment: GE's tax department has been estimated to employ 975 people, not to mention its lobbyists (Kocieniewski 2011a). (3) *Low taxation for wealthy Americans.* Many of the richest Americans have been able to maneuver their annual earnings into lower-taxed capital gains. During the 2012 presidential campaign, Mitt Romney was forced to admit that he paid 13.9 percent on his $21.7 million gross income for 2010. The federal tax rate for the four hundred Americans with the highest incomes fell from 30 percent to 17 percent between 1995 and 2007, to the point where Warren Buffet, one of the richest people in America, published a *New York Times* commentary (August 19, 2011) asking the government to raise taxes on the rich. He claimed to pay only 17.4 percent of his taxable income to the federal government in 2010, less than all the other people in his office, who averaged 36 percent. "My [billion-aire] friends and I have been coddled long enough." Most of those friends, however, remained silent. Collins (2012) has referred to this kind of thing as "a triumph of capital and a betrayal of work" (p. 8).

59. Back then, de Tocqueville wrote, "Democracy has . . . been abandoned to its wild interests, and it has grown up like those children who have no parental guidance" (1840/2003: 7). He was talking about France, not America. About America, he wrote, "[D]uring my stay in the United States, nothing struck me more forcefully than the general equality of condition among the people" (p. 3).

60. One study of health care in the most developed Western countries (Davis, Schoen, and Stremikis 2010) found that the United States ranked last on the dimensions of access, patient safety, coordination, efficiency, and equality. Infant mortality and mortality amenable to health care were the highest among the developed nations. A 2006 study found the rates of diabetes and heart disease among the wealthiest and best-educated Americans to be comparable with those of the poorest and least-educated English. Yet the most popular prescription for fixing American health care continues to

be treating it more as a business and increasing its level of competition (see, for example, Porter and Teisberg 2004, 2006; also Herzlinger 2006, 2007), even though American health care is already highly competitive and business-like. (This topic is discussed at length in a book I am completing entitled *Managing the Myths of Health Care*.)

61. For more on "America's Great Regression" (in relation to the discussion of income disparities that follows), see Reich (2011).

62. For the human side of these numbers, see Putnam's (2013) description of the lives of haves and have-nots in the Ohio town of his youth, compared with those living in that town today.

63. For a list of overt U.S. military and covert CIA interventions, see "From Wounded Knee to Libya: A Century of U.S. Military Interventions" (Grossman 2012). The Monroe Doctrine, issued in 1823 to stop European interference in the newly liberated countries of Latin America, eventually metamorphosed into an America declaration of dependence: the country's self-appointed right to intervene unilaterally in any country of the Western Hemisphere, and later the world, that acted contrary to its own interests.

64. "Somewhere in the back of their minds, a lot of people seem to be realizing that the alternative to a United States–dominated world . . . is a leaderless world" (Friedman 2009). "To regain the identity it enjoyed during the Cold War, the United States ought to become the leader of a community of democracies. . . . [It] would still need to retain its military might, but this strength would serve to protect a just world order" (Soros 2004: 167–168).

65. Here, too, denial is the order of the day. In one of his recent columns, entitled "Saving the System," David Brooks (2014b) wrote, "Powerful people have generally tried to impose their version of the Truth on less powerful people." He was referring to other powerful people, without recognizing (in this column, at least) that what he called "liberal pluralism" is his and America's version of the Truth. Five weeks later

(2014a), Brooks quoted Micklethwait and Wooldridge (2014) that "so far, the 21st Century has been a rotten one for the Western model," while in an earlier column (2011c), he wrote about the "vertiginous tangle" of interests overwhelming the U.S. government." Brooks seems to be of two minds: recognizing what is going on locally yet blind to some of its consequences globally.

66. As this book was being finalized for publication, new threats were appearing: Russia was back to cold war habits in Ukraine, and ISIS was carrying extremism to new levels of barbarism in the Middle East. Do we need to rely on "liberal democracy," led by America, after all? In a *New York Times* "Letter from America," Anand Giridharadas (2014) came to another conclusion, consistent with the arguments of this book:

> Behind the chaos is a void of influence right now—a void in which countries are unable to prevent other countries or ragamuffin groups from doing bad things. And behind the void of influence is a void of example. . . . By failing to embody so many of its own ideals nowadays, the United States (like other liberal democracies) deprives the world of a compelling counterweight to the ideas (such as they are) of so-called Putinism, ISISism, Islamism, Chinese authoritarianism and other -isms on the march. In this liquid, interdependent age, many people around the world wonder what to believe in.

About This Endeavor

I AM CANADIAN, born and raised in Montreal. I was educated in mechanical engineering at McGill University and took my first job out of college at the Canadian National Railway. Graduate studies in management followed, at MIT in Boston, and then I returned to McGill, where I have been researching, writing, and educating about management and organizations ever since—educating in recent years, especially in our unusual International Masters in Practicing Management (www.impm.org), International Masters for Health Leadership (www.imhl.org), and an enterprise called CoachingOurselves.com. During this time, I also spent eight years abroad, with stints in France, Switzerland, England, and the Czech Republic. (Details on all this can be found at www.mintzberg.org.)

So who am I to be doing this?

After all, I am not an expert on most of the issues discussed here. But given the scope of all of them together, who is? Experts specialize, with the consequence that the big problems get lost in specialized writings, or else get distorted when viewed through a single lens. Yet there are significant insights in these writings that need to be brought into some kind of comprehensive framework, alongside what we can see for ourselves in this troubled world. And that is where I can claim some expertise: my most successful books have synthesized ideas from a variety of sources.

To the best of my recollection, I began to think about this framework twenty-three years ago, when I visited Prague soon after the collapse of communism in Eastern Europe. The popular explanation for this collapse—that capitalism had triumphed—struck me then as not only wrong but also dangerous. A year later I published an article that discussed the triumph of balance in terms of three sectors of society and warned about the risk of losing that balance (Mintzberg 1992; see also 2002). These concerns have hardly diminished in the ensuing years.

I began to collect materials—many books and articles, all kinds of scribbled notes—and asked people in places I visited to organize small workshops to discuss the evolving framework. From 2001 to 2014, we held twenty-four of these, all over the world.[1]

In 2009, I opened the several boxes of materials that I had collected. After struggling through about fifteen drafts, I posted *Rebalancing Society* as an "electronic pamphlet" on www.mintzberg.org in February 2014. This book is a revision of that pamphlet, with the same title (and it joins that pamphlet on my website, thanks to a publisher who practices what this book preaches). To keep this version as short as possible, I have removed some material that

---

[1] The first took place in New Zealand, and subsequent ones were held in London, Costa Rica, Brittany, Ghana, Beijing, Mexico City, Prague, Nairobi, Tuscany, the United States (the World Bank in Washington, D.C, the New School in New York, the Darden School at the University of Virginia, and a conference of the Academy of Management), Canada (Vancouver, Ottawa, St. Jerome and Ste. Marguerite, Quebec, and with the Sauvé Scholars at McGill), and more recently in Lima, Paris, Tokyo, and, finally, two at the McGill University Desautels Faculty of Management.

can be accessed in the original pamphlet (including a fuller rendition of the appendix, which appears there on pages 79–106).

Where do I go from here? I keep working on some of these ideas and hope to post whatever comes of that on my website (but I have no idea when that will be, so please don't ask!). What I can say now is that colleagues and I at McGill are doing a GROOC—a MOOC (massive open online course) for groups—entitled "Social Learning for Social Impact," which is scheduled to appear on edX in September 2015 (see https://www.mcgill.ca/desautels/programs/grooc). I have also started a TWOG—from tweet2blog—accessible via Twitter @Mintzberg141, or directly at mintzberg.org that shares "rousing reflections in a page or two instead of pithy pronouncements in a sentence or two" delving into all kinds of issues, including the rebalancing of society.

Special Appreciation

My stints abroad have significantly shaped this effort, but perhaps of greater influence has been my good fortune in being raised in, and continuing to enjoy, a city as vibrant as Montreal, in a province as human as Quebec, in a country that has been as balanced as Canada.[2] No less influential has been my academic life at McGill, a university that remains scholarly in the best sense of the term. These are wonderful places from which to reflect on the big issues of our day, especially as they are manifested in our powerful neighbor. Canadians live close enough to the United States to be able to understand Americans

---

[2] Mihaela Firsirotu, Yvan Allaire, and I have been working on a book entitled *Canadians on Balance* that draws together the writings of many Canadians on social, political, and economic issues.

rather well yet distant enough to be able to see things a little differently.

A special thank-you for help provided, pronouncements corrected, and comments suggested—especially to Bill Litwack, for finding big conceptual improvements and little grammatical errors, and José Carlos Marques, for filling in so many of the blanks and flagging a number of significant weaknesses, plus Gui Azevedo and Rennie Nilsson who played a similar role in earlier stages. Also for various useful suggestions to Farzad Khan, Alvaro Bermejo, Alan Engelstad, Fred Bird, Sasha Sadilova, Brian King, Tana Paddock, Dulcie Naimer, my daughters Susie and Lisa, Rabbi Ron Aigen (for a sermon in September 2010 from which I borrowed the title *Radical Renewal*[3]), and the many thoughtful people who participated in the workshops. An insightful conference organized by Allen White of the Tellus Institute in 2013 (www.corporation2020.org) led me to write Chapter 4 (just when I believed I was finally finished!). John Breitner came up with a number of incisive suggestions, including one that led to "the John question." My appreciation as well to Irene Piorkowski, who asked the question that bears her name in the text. Mary Plawutsky, Nic Albert, and Laura Larson came in near the end to clean things up and Michael Bass to get this into production, while Nina Coutinho, Tatiana Saliba, Karl Moore, Ron Duerksen, Chris Chipello, and Leilani Ku worked diligently to get the word out on the pamphlet.

Once again, only more so this time, I have been delighted to work with Berrett-Koehler, an island of sanity and benevolence in the mad world of publishing. If ever a book fit with a publisher, this is it.

---

[3] The title is in reference to the historical Jewish Jubilee, where every fifty years society was given the possibility of starting over again.

About This Endeavor

Finally, a special thank-you to Santa Balanca-Rodrigues, not only for toiling through all those drafts (since mostly I write *off* key), but also for managing to keep the rest of my work life on track with her usual delightful nature.

Berrett–Koehler
Publishers

Berrett-Koehler is an independent publisher dedicated to an ambitious mission: *connecting people and ideas to create a world that works for all.*

We believe that to truly create a better world, action is needed at all levels—individual, organizational, and societal. At the individual level, our publications help people align their lives with their values and with their aspirations for a better world. At the organizational level, our publications promote progressive leadership and management practices, socially responsible approaches to business, and humane and effective organizations. At the societal level, our publications advance social and economic justice, shared prosperity, sustainability, and new solutions to national and global issues.

A major theme of our publications is "Opening Up New Space." Berrett-Koehler titles challenge conventional thinking, introduce new ideas, and foster positive change. Their common quest is changing the underlying beliefs, mindsets, institutions, and structures that keep generating the same cycles of problems, no matter who our leaders are or what improvement programs we adopt.

We strive to practice what we preach—to operate our publishing company in line with the ideas in our books. At the core of our approach is stewardship, which we define as a deep sense of responsibility to administer the company for the benefit of all of our "stakeholder" groups: authors, customers, employees, investors, service providers, and the communities and environment around us.

We are grateful to the thousands of readers, authors, and other friends of the company who consider themselves to be part of the "BK Community." We hope that you, too, will join us in our mission.

A BK Currents Book

This book is part of our BK Currents series. BK Currents books advance social and economic justice by exploring the critical intersections between business and society. Offering a unique combination of thoughtful analysis and progressive alternatives, BK Currents books promote positive change at the national and global levels. To find out more, visit **www.bkconnection.com**.

Berrett–Koehler
Publishers

Connecting people and ideas
to create a world that works for all

Dear Reader,

Thank you for picking up this book and joining our worldwide community of Berrett-Koehler readers. We share ideas that bring positive change into people's lives, organizations, and society.

To welcome you, we'd like to offer you a free e-book. You can pick from among twelve of our bestselling books by entering the promotional code **BKP92E** here: http://www.bkconnection.com/welcome.

When you claim your free e-book, we'll also send you a copy of our e-newsletter, the *BK Communiqué*. Although you're free to unsubscribe, there are many benefits to sticking around. In every issue of our newsletter you'll find

- A free e-book
- Tips from famous authors
- Discounts on spotlight titles
- Hilarious insider publishing news
- A chance to win a prize for answering a riddle

Best of all, our readers tell us, "Your newsletter is the only one I actually read." So claim your gift today, and please stay in touch!

Sincerely,

Charlotte Ashlock
Steward of the BK Website

Questions? Comments? Contact me at bkcommunity@bkpub.com.

Certified Sourcing
www.sfiprogram.org
SFI-00453

Certified

Corporation
bcorporation.net